About Island Press

Since 1984, the nonprofit organization Island Press has been stimulating, shaping, and communicating ideas that are essential for solving environmental problems worldwide. With more than 1,000 titles in print and some 30 new releases each year, we are the nation's leading publisher on environmental issues. We identify innovative thinkers and emerging trends in the environmental field. We work with world-renowned experts and authors to develop cross-disciplinary solutions to environmental challenges.

Island Press designs and executes educational campaigns, in conjunction with our authors, to communicate their critical messages in print, in person, and online using the latest technologies, innovative programs, and the media. Our goal is to reach targeted audiences—scientists, policy makers, environmental advocates, urban planners, the media, and concerned citizens—with information that can be used to create the framework for long-term ecological health and human well-being.

Island Press gratefully acknowledges major support from The Bobolink Foundation, Caldera Foundation, The Curtis and Edith Munson Foundation, The Forrest C. and Frances H. Lattner Foundation, The JPB Foundation, The Kresge Foundation, The Summit Charitable Foundation, Inc., and many other generous organizations and individuals.

The opinions expressed in this book are those of the author(s) and do not necessarily reflect the views of our supporters.

At the Table

At the Table

THE CHEF'S GUIDE TO ADVOCACY

Katherine Miller

ISLANDPRESS | Washington | Covelo

Library of Congress Control Number: 2023934536

All Island Press books are printed on
environmentally responsible materials.

Manufactured in the United States of America

10 9 8 7 6 5 4 3 2 1

Keywords: Certified B Corporation; Chef Action Network; Chef Bootcamp for Policy and Change; Chefs Collaborative; environmental impacts of food; farm to table; farmworkers; food insecurity; Food Policy Action; food waste; hunger relief; Independent Restaurant Coalition; James Beard Foundation; National Restaurant Association; restaurant aid; restaurant industry; sustainable agriculture; sustainable seafood; tipped minimum wage; waitstaff

For Gracie, Tessa, Katherine, and Samantha:
Use your voice.

Contents

Foreword

by Chef Tanya Holland

As a young chef, I trained in a brigade system in which the head chef ruled. Working in near silence, I perfected mother sauces, learned to dress pheasants, and cut thousands of basil leaves into delicate chiffonade. In those days, professional kitchens were exclusively the domain of white men. We, all the students, wore the same chef whites, carried similar knives, and put up with military-style hazing considered part of our culinary training. As a Black woman, I was regularly harassed—sometimes with microaggressions, sometimes with more extreme and unique forms of abuse. Pitched as a way to bring order to the chaos of restaurant kitchens, the brigade system was—and still is—the prevailing way chefs are trained.

The only thing that matters in the old way of teaching is the preservation and proliferation of cooking techniques. Not until many years later did I understand that professional cooking didn't come automatically coupled with jokes mocking my Blackness or with sexually explicit gestures. As I grew into being a chef, into being a leader—first in restaurants and then as the host of the first cooking show helmed by a Black woman and successful restaurateur, and now as a member of the board of trustees of the James

Beard Foundation—I was, and am, constantly processing and unlearning the lessons of the past.

It isn't easy. Even decades after I first entered cooking school, I still often find myself the only woman (and certainly the only Black woman) at the tables where knowledge is shared and decisions are made. That's because societal and cultural barriers block me, and others like me, from access to certain opportunities. It's also because structural racism and white supremacy exist in every facet of our society and are baked into the policies that govern our food system.

Becoming more and more aware of the structural flaws that prevent change, I knew that I wanted to do something about it. I am not a shy person, and I have never been scared to use my voice. In the past, however, I wasn't particularly successful at changing things. In some cases, I thought people didn't hear what I had to say no matter how forcefully I was saying it. One chef accused me of "playing the race card" when I approached him about obviously being treated differently by the sous chefs who clearly had racial and gender biases. The old ways felt caked on, and progress moves too slowly for my liking. And my self-preservation and awareness were perceived as defensive and whiny.

Women chefs and restaurateurs, even after the MeToo years and dozens of programs designed to change the game, still earn less than our male counterparts. We still get less than 10 percent of investment capital when we open restaurants. Without outside capital, it is hard for small restaurants to grow and for our brands to grow. I was hosting my own cooking show on Oprah Winfrey's OWN network, but the only way to save my restaurant from predatory partners and financing was to shut it down.

The societal flaws that exacerbated the closing of my business aren't new. The same racism and systemic bias exist in efforts to reduce emergency hunger programs such as the school lunch and the Supplemental Nutrition Assistance Program. Lawsuits that blocked the Small Business Administration's ability to prioritize restaurants owned by women or people of color for special loans during COVID-19 were similar to those filed against the United States Department of Agriculture to prevent Black farmers from accessing funds to buy farmland.

Today, I know that one of the most powerful things we can do is to fight for policy changes at the state and federal levels. As a business owner, but most importantly as a vocal constituent, I have experience that matters in the rooms where policy is written. My voice, connections, and public platform can help accelerate change in my community.

That's something I always knew, but I never quite had the formula down until I attended a training program put on by the Chef Action Network and James Beard Foundation at TomKat Ranch in California in 2016. It was there I first met Katherine Miller, along with many other chefs from Northern California, including a few who worked just a few miles from my restaurant but I had never met. At this regional Chef Bootcamp for Policy and Change, I truly learned that with the right recipe, I could cook up change.

During those three days, we went through an early version of the "A Is for Advocacy" training contained in this book. We participated in role-plays on how to talk to elected officials, toured the farm, and cooked together. I built powerful relationships within the chef and restaurant community. Most importantly, I learned valuable advocacy skills that I still use today. The training also helped expand my appetite for change. I was so locked into fighting for equity and inclusion in the industry—and still am—that I hadn't truly seen how connected our food system is to almost every other aspect of our lives. From who grows our food to who serves it, our individual actions can support—or bring down—the system that controls us.

At the end of that weekend, I started getting more deeply involved with organizations such as No Kid Hungry. Universal school meals are a human right, and we've passed a law that codifies that right in California. Climate change is threatening our very existence. Chefs across the United States are working to raise awareness about regenerative agriculture and healthy soils. Also, in my home state of California, we passed a law to provide new funding for farmers who use more cover crops and climate-friendly growing techniques.

Change can take a long time, but I saw how quickly policy can affect our daily lives when, shortly after returning from TomKat, I joined the campaign to implement a tax on sugary drinks and soda in Oakland. Sugar-laden beverages are proven to contribute to diet-related diseases—diseases that disproportionately impact the Black community. We passed our soda tax in 2016, and today it is considered a successful model for improving diets and reducing disease rates in the city.

There is nothing easy about these issues, but thanks in part to Katherine's guidance, I can now translate complicated issues around food and make them tangible and actionable for others. It's a skill that I have honed over decades of working in kitchens. It's a skill I share with my fellow chefs. It is also, like all knives, a skill that needs to be regularly sharpened. The work I did with Katherine helped me develop an approach and strategy that worked for me. I feel empowered to impact change in my community.

The tips, tools, and tactics from that training stay with me and inform many of the decisions I make about what issues I'm going to take on and exactly how I want to work. I use the advice described throughout this book almost every day. I know you will find it equally useful.

I also need to say a word about Katherine. I entered that first training not knowing anything about her. Starting when she was the first vice president of impact at the James Beard Foundation, Katherine and I have worked together to strategize everything from launching my cookbook to the Farm Bill. After years of traveling the country with her, including to other trainings, and while walking the halls of Congress, I have come to respect her knowledge and experience about advocacy. This book is your chance to tap into her decades of experience crisscrossing food, politics, and policy and then apply what you learn to your own work.

Katherine also lays out some of the most pressing challenges we face as a culinary community—and as citizens of the world. The word *chef* means leader. Too often, it has meant being a boss or dictator. not a mentor or champion. That changes now. It's time we're known for more than delicious and precious food. What you'll find in *At the Table* will help guide you and introduce you to new ways of doing business.

I look forward to seeing what you do with tools here and how you will change the world.

About Tanya Holland

Holland is a chef, restaurateur, podcast host, writer, and a renowned expert on soul food. The author of the recently released *Tanya Holland's California Soul*, *The Brown Sugar Kitchen Cookbook*, and *New Soul Cooking*, Holland competed on the fifteenth season of *Top Chef* on Bravo, was the host and soul-food expert on Food Network's *Melting Pot Soul Kitchen*, appeared on the HBO Max show *Selena + Chef* featuring Selena Gomez, and hosted *Tanya's Kitchen Table* on Oprah Winfrey's OWN Network. She is a member of the James Beard Foundation's board of trustees and the esteemed Les Dames d'Escoffier organizations, as well as a senior advisor to the Stanford (University) Food Institute.

Chapter 1

The Power of Chefs

I consider myself an advocate. I take the time to
learn about the things I care about, and then I use
my voice so that others can learn more and join in.
We can't change anything if we don't do something.
—*Chef-author Kwame Onwuachi*[1]

In 2012 chef Michel Nischan and entrepreneur Eric
Kessler approached me to help them design and lead a
training focused on turning chefs into political advocates.
At first, this idea seemed the most ludicrous thing I had ever
heard. It also seemed frivolous and unnecessary. I remember thinking—and probably saying—that those chefs and
restaurateurs were probably best left in the kitchen. After
all, how is a group of people better known for their tattoos,
tempers, and television appearances going to have a real
impact in politics and the halls of Congress? No one was
going to take them seriously, I thought.

Don't misunderstand me: I love restaurants. For years I
considered myself a "foodie," admiring chefs, following who

was opening which restaurant and where, and devouring any and all media featuring chefs, from the latest competition to their fashion choices. Restaurants are cool: the physical spaces, the people that work in them, the food they prepare, and the creativity and entrepreneurship that is present in every single restaurant, whether it is a neighborhood café or a place where one set of table linens costs more than my car payment. I also believe that food is art, and restaurants and bars are where I find modernists, classics, and everything in between. The booths, tables, and barstools of the world's restaurants are where I've celebrated most of life's milestones—birthdays, signing mortgage papers, ending relationships, starting new jobs, getting married. They are places where I created space for big conversations, made important memories, and shared the love and wisdom of family and friends. They are also places where I got to come face to face with my culinary idols.

Despite my love of these spaces, and my fangirl moments, I never really thought of chefs and restaurants as leaders, activists, or advocates. For me, restaurants were places to extract beauty, deliciousness, warmth, and friendship. My gratitude for their work was expressed with a big tip, a hearty thanks, and a return visit.

I considered my own work in a vastly different sphere. Since the 1990s, I've traveled the world working with activists and advocates in hopes of helping them use their voices to make real progress in the areas of climate change, gender equity, sexual violence, and global health. For a long time, though, I did not see what was right in front of me: that all these issues are intimately connected to food.

Like most consumers, I thought of food as, well, just food. I came to realize that food is one of our most personal and political daily acts. Too many in the food world—especially in restaurants—focus on flavor first (and often exclusively). Our food choices, though, affect more than just our stomachs. Our food choices impact everything from our personal health to the preservation of the planet.

Understanding the connection between our plates, personal preferences, and the politics governing our food system feels both obvious and challenging. Too often, we focus on the plate because it's easier to talk about how fresh blueberries taste than it is to talk about how they were grown and harvested (often by underage and undocumented farmworkers). When we exchange recipes for shrimp tacos, we can simply ignore the discussion around whether the shrimp was raised in polluted farm waters or caught by third-generation shrimpers or if the corn for the tortillas was genetically modified (more than 90 percent of all corn grown in the United States is,[2] by the way).

We have to start looking beyond our own plates and preferences and see what our choices are doing to our communities. The policies, choices, and trade-offs holding up our current food system are inextricably linked—and not always in a good way.

Nowhere is this clearer for me than global meat consumption. The first time I saw a live animal slaughter, as part of the first Chef Bootcamp for Policy and Change, I better understood the issues in front of us. If we choose to eat meat, there are dozens of questions we need to, as consumers, ask ourselves. Was the animal raised by a small family farmer who doesn't use feed that includes additional antibiotics, or was it bought from a large multinational company that relies on concentrated animal feeding operations, or CAFOs, to keep up with global demand? Was it processed on a small farm, or was it sent to a slaughterhouse where millions of pounds of meat are processed each day? Were the workers on the farms, in the slaughterhouses, and in the grocery stores all paid a living wage, free of harassment and violence, and were they able to access health care and other benefits? How much are we willing to pay for products that are in sync with our personal values?

To a consumer, these questions can be overwhelming. Each answer leads to another question, and every decision feels like the wrong choice. It all leads, very quickly, to information paralysis, and when faced with so many choices, we often default to the status quo—the thing that takes the least amount of effort and thought. That stand is no longer acceptable. Consumers, companies, and yes, even chefs need help understanding our food system and finding ways to improve it.

I believe we all must work to ensure that the food we eat is delicious but is also good for us and the planet. That's where chefs come in. Chefs can help translate what goes into producing our food to what is on our dinner table—and can help us all understand how food policy, from cottage food laws to global fishery management treaties, affects what is available to us and at what cost.

The laws that control our food system are often intentionally opaque. For example, did you know that there is no single, federal food agency? Before starting this work, I didn't. Now after a decade of working on food policy advocacy, I know that (at least) twenty federal departments and agencies play some role in shaping our food system. Take food safety, for example, which is notoriously convoluted in how it is governed. At least thirty federal laws touch on the issue of food safety. Although fifteen federal agencies play some part in implementing these laws, the regulation of food safety largely falls on the US Food and Drug Administration (FDA) and the US Department of Agriculture (USDA).[3] But the division of authority between the two is not always neat.

Let's use eggs as an example. USDA runs a marketing program promoting eggs and regulates the safety of eggs removed from the shell. At the same time, another agency, the FDA regulates the safety of eggs inside the shell. To get from the chicken to the farmer to you, eggs will have successfully navigated dozens of laws overseeing their production and making sure they land safely (in every way) on your plate.

Even though there are dozens of laws around food safety and production, the system does not bring the same urgency to ensuring that food jobs pay fair wages, support local economies, or try to address climate change. To create change, we must work to unravel and rewrite hundreds of years of public policies that perpetuate the racism, sexism, wage discrimination, and environmental degradation that is baked into the way food is produced, sold, and distributed.

Even as I became more aware of the need to reform the food system, I didn't think of the restaurant industry as part of the solution, partly because restaurants are a major part of the problem. The food system in which most restaurant owners and chefs (and their purveyors) work functions exactly how it was designed: it delivers cheap,

calorically dense, and convenient food to the largest number of people possible without real concern for the people
or planet that deliver our food. (Let's be clear: there is
always a difference between small, independent restaurants
and large, multinational chains, but they all must mostly
operate within the same flawed system.)

Still, many restaurant workers express pride in being
part of an industry where "anyone" can get a job. Restaurant work is often sold as a place for those who do not
necessarily fit into other industries or companies to grow
and succeed. The hip and cool factor masks many of the
endemic problems within the industry. Only about one-
third of restaurants are owned by women, less than 10 percent of head chefs are women, and the numbers are even
worse for owners of color.[4] It is also a place that—with
shift drinks, long hours, and a work-hard, play-hard
vibe—fosters some of the highest rates of drug and alcohol addiction and suicide of any profession. That restaurants are still able to create delicious meals and meaningful
experiences is a testament to the dogged personality and
creativity of the people who own them and work in them.
But it was not an industry I was looking to for inspiration
or counting on to drive change.

I wasn't alone in these feelings. Food justice activists
have been skeptical of the chef and restaurant community's commitment to social change for years. The largest
industry group, the National Restaurant Association (and
before 2020 the only national lobbying group representing
restaurants), actively fought against the Affordable Care
Act ("Obama Care")[5] and state and national efforts to raise
the minimum wage.[6] I've been told, numerous times by

leaders I admire, that until chefs clean up their act and run fairer businesses, they have no real place in the good food movement.

I don't entirely disagree. I spent more than a decade directing opposition research efforts for the Democratic Party. I know that if you're going to speak out about issues, you better clean up your own kitchen first.

That cleanup takes time—and it is complicated. Some of the chefs and restaurateurs I know provide health care and other benefits for their employees, pay above the minimum wage, and look for meaningful ways to engage in their communities, but often they are anomalies in their industry. Most restaurateurs struggle to simply keep the doors open. The business model is broken: wages are low; sexism, racism, and sexual harassment are rampant; the hours are insane and ingredients increasingly expensive. The profit margins, if you're lucky, run between 3 and 10 percent annually.[7] At this time, there are few financial incentives for chefs and restaurant owners to source from local businesses, provide health care, or pay a livable wage. There are demands and expectations that these small business owners provide all the protections and benefits of larger corporations, but they are trapped by myriad opaque laws, age-old practices, and financial considerations that hinder their efforts to clean up their kitchens and the industry. For too long these traps have been used as excuses, but I'm hoping they now provide motivation for change.

Despite the institutional challenges they face, what Nischan and Kessler knew (and I realized) is that chefs are uniquely positioned to spur big-picture change in their industry and in the larger debates around the future of our food system.

In other words, chefs are a key ingredient in making not just restaurants, but the food system itself, more just and sustainable. They influence what we grow and produce and how we eat, and they shape almost every conversation we have about food, from the fun (trending flavors) to the serious (exploitation of workers). They have a deep knowledge of the business and economics of the food system and influence culture through social media, television, and books. They have expansive networks and unprecedented access to politicians and other influencers. Most importantly, there is strong demand for them to step out of the kitchen—especially from other food systems advocates who understand their reach and influence.

Recipe for Making Effective Advocates

Required ingredients: Cultural influence, economic clout, unique networks, direct access, trusted voice, powerful storytellers, demand for your voice

Proportions may vary.

Mix generously and apply often to causes and issues you care about.

Like It or Not, Chefs Are Celebrities (and Influence Culture)

One of the first things that Kessler said to me when pitching the idea of a Chef Bootcamp was that chefs are, for better or worse, cultural influencers and celebrities. He shared his experience collaborating with musicians and other artists and how through training and education, global icons such as Bono had become trusted partners in discussions about global poverty reduction. He thought the same was possible for so-called celebrity chefs.

He wasn't—and isn't—wrong to compare chefs to musicians and other artists. Food is a dominant part of our entertainment culture. Chefs have more followers and fans on social media than they are likely to ever have customers, and television, blogs, and newsletters reach billions more. Just consider the following:

- There are more than 3.6 billion social media accounts in the world, and more than half of the top shared content is focused on food.[8]
- Nearly four million unique users visit the top 160 food blogs each month.[9]
- Nearly 80 percent of Americans watch cooking shows,[10] and all the major streaming platforms—Amazon Prime, Netflix, Hulu—create and showcase food in everything from documentaries to classic cooking shows to the craziest of food contests.
- The Food Network is distributed to nearly one hundred million US households (or 87 percent) and draws more than forty-six million unique web users monthly.[11]
- In 2021, chef and food personality Guy Fieri signed a production deal with the Food Network worth more than $80 million. Compared to contracts for

professional athletes, Fieri's deal was the equivalent of a top contract in the National Football League.[12]

Chefs can reach more people through television and social media than almost any other group or organization. Chef Andrea Reusing, known for her restaurant Lantern in Chapel Hill, North Carolina, said it best: "I was an activist before I was a chef, and my decision to cook was as much about politics and making change as it was food."[13]

Restaurants Support Economies in Every City

Having worked with members of Congress and governors across the United States, one thing that struck me early on about chefs was that they, more than other advocates, could speak to their industry's direct contribution to the economy. Restaurants are one of the few employment sectors that have a presence in almost every US city. There are more than one million restaurant locations. They include quick-serve, chain, and independent restaurants, and they make the industry one of the country's top employment sectors. Consumers spend nearly 40 percent (36.7 percent) of their food dollars in restaurants—this money pays for others to host, prepare, and serve our meals, and clean up afterward.[14]

From small diners to fast-food franchises to fine dining, restaurants are integral to our communities and support economic growth and development. According to a US restaurant industry white paper published in 2020:

In addition to contributing significantly to the more than $760 billion [about $2,300 per person in the United States] in annual sales in the broader restaurant economy, these restaurants directly employ 11 million people [about twice the population of Arizona] across the country. Nearly three million of these jobs were created in just the last decade. . . . Further, as mainstays of regional, local, and ethnic cuisine, independent restaurants also drive domestic and international travel and tourism to all parts of the country, from big cities (e.g., Miami) to smaller locales (e.g., Portland, Maine). Food culture and food tourism have become ingrained in the American economy and underpin the travel, leisure, and hospitality sector. Foreign and domestic travelers spend hundreds of billions annually in US restaurants ($279 billion [about $860 per person in the United States] in 2019).[15]

The industry is also responsible for another five million jobs, including dairies, farmers, fisheries, and other producers, which together accounted for more than $900 billion (about $2,800 per person in the United States) annually in direct sales in 2019.[16] Although the industry took a significant hit in both earnings and jobs as a result of the COVID-19 pandemic—earnings in 2020 were down by about $200 billion (about $620 per person in the United States), and about one million jobs were lost between March 2020 and September 2021[17]—forecasters predict that restaurants and food service will continue to be an area for economic growth for years to come.[18]

The restaurant industry employs hundreds of people and generates millions in local revenue. The chefs, owners, leaders, and staff are exactly the communities and constituents that should be in conversation with policy makers and legislators.

Chefs' Networks Are Unique and Powerful

In the food system, few people are as well connected and naturally networked as a chef or restaurant owner. Chefs have most of the attributes sociology experts point to as signs of highly networked individuals, including "a genuine interest in other people, a desire to help others, patience, a future-focused mindset, and a focus on quality over quantity."[19] Most would agree that except for patience, these are also common personality traits for a successful chef or restaurateur.

Think of a network as the table you're trying to set. Everyone you meet has the potential to sit at the table and help you advance the issues you care about.

"One reason that chef voices matter so much, in whatever battles we are fighting, is that we have amazing and very different networks—networks of people and communities that haven't in the past had a voice in the way things are run," said chef-owner Jamilka Borges of Pittsburgh's Wild Child. "Whether it's our own personal networks, our customers, our employees, our producers/ vendors, or our fellow chefs—we bring those relationships to our lives and work. It's one of our biggest superpowers. Once I dug into my contacts and thought about my networks and circles of influence, it really made me realize that I actually have a lot of power to leverage."[20]

Networks consist of everyone from employees to customers to media to fans and followers to suppliers and vendors to investors—every person a chef touches over the course of a day.

Chefs—especially so-called celebrity chefs—are the ones that most guests come to see or sample their dishes.

Most guests would love to meet the chef, visit the chef, and take a selfie. In-demand restaurants attract high-level guests, including mayors, entertainers, governors, and even presidents. Chefs and restaurants are also at the center of their community, both as active participants in fundraisers and unique events and as gathering places on Main Streets or downtown.

In addition to their individual networks, chefs are also able to tap into the connections and relationships of other chefs. It all adds up to the ability to influence culture, in new and powerful ways.

Working with others within your network helps present a unified message to policy makers and proves that the issue is important to others in your community. The more people you have repeating the same message, the bigger the chance of success. The more networked you are and the more you ask your community to join you, the more power you're building to help shift policies, practices, and thinking on the issues you care about.

Asha Gomez, a chef and restaurateur from Atlanta, works extensively on global hunger and food insecurity issues. She uses her platform to raise awareness around global hunger and food insecurity—systemic problems that she first learned about when she adopted her son, Ethan, from an orphanage in India when he was four years old. Ethan was severely malnourished, and it took several years for Gomez to feed him back to health. During that time, she learned more about the issues affecting the global food supply and was frustrated by her own inability to influence change.

"I went through so much of my life wanting to make a difference but not knowing how to impact change, and

I've come to realize that my voice matters. I can affect change just by bringing awareness to certain issues near and dear to me, to my restaurants, to the people that I interact with, to the community that I live in, work in, and play in," Gomez explained. "These conversations that we have around our dinner tables with friends and family and our guests that come to our restaurant create the change. I can have a real impact on ending global hunger, a problem that impacted my son, by using my voice and my connections. These conversations we can bring to the halls of Congress."[21]

Direct Access to Policy Makers

Chefs, restaurant owners, and hospitality workers have greater access to their governors, members of Congress, and even the president of the United States than almost any other community leaders. If you ask a group of chefs and culinary professionals whether an elected official or candidate has visited their business, everyone raises their hand. When you ask how often those officials stop in, many respond that it is at least once a month and sometimes more often.

This interaction creates a special relationship between chefs and restaurant owners and can make it easier to reach out to an elected official or their staff about critical issues. A few years ago, Seattle chef and restaurateur Renee Erickson went to Washington, DC, to meet with members of Congress about the bill that regulates marine fisheries in US waters, the Magnuson-Stevens Act. The organization she was working with had told her that it was unable to secure a meeting with Maria Cantwell, one of Erickson's Washington senators. As Erickson was walking through the halls from one building to another, the senator saw her and asked her why she was in town. The two held an impromptu meeting in the hallway, and it turned out that Cantwell was a regular at Erickson's restaurants.

"She comes into the restaurants all the time. We are in regular contact with her and her staff. It just didn't occur to me to ask her for fifteen minutes of her time when I was in DC. Turns out, she supported the bill and later voted for it. She understood what it meant to Washington fisheries and restaurants," said Erickson.[22]

The ability to access politicians and elected officials also works because, since the beginning of American democracy, they have understood the power of food to signal their values and personality.

George Washington offered voters gallons of alcohol during his first campaign for the Virginia House of Burgesses. Massive political barbecues across New York State were used to sway voters with oxen feasts in the early 1900s. Today, it is illegal in most states to give voters free food or alcohol in return for a vote, but that doesn't stop politicians and elected officials from hosting fundraisers at restaurants, popping into a bar for a quick beer and photo op, or getting together with friends and family at carefully chosen restaurants.[23]

Vice President Kamala Harris often signals her personal values and politics through food. She and her husband, Douglas Emhoff, dine regularly at local restaurants, favoring spots run by women and owned by people of color. During the 2020 presidential campaign, she made dosas with actress Mindy Kaling, and in July 2019, before the Democratic debate in Detroit, she dropped by chef April Anderson's Good Cakes and Bakes.[24]

By choosing Good Cakes and Bakes, a shop owned by a Black-Queer woman, Harris sent a strong message about her own commitment to entrepreneurs and women leaders. She continued this practice during her first year in the White House when she hosted a roundtable of Latina business leaders, including Daniella Senior, founder and owner of Colada Shop in the DC metropolitan area.[25] Focusing on food gives politicians the ability to talk about jobs and the economy, and restaurants and businesses provide the perfect setting for political theater.

In Food We Trust

Food holds a complex place in our lives. It's both emotional and rational, personal and public. How food affects our health, reflects our values, and contributes to our mood and personal economics directly overlaps and intersects with a variety of issues, including public policy and marketing to shape the view and relationship with food. Chefs are often able to navigate this complicated landscape because of the inherent trust that consumers (and others) place in the food system.

Think about it: trust is a crucial element of working in a professional kitchen. Kitchens are dangerous environments, and trusted relationships help everyone navigate hot oil, sharp knives, and boiling water. Trust is equally important in advocacy, where words and actions will be part of the public record.

Each year, a global public affairs company, Edelman, publishes the Global Trust Barometer. Since 2012, when I first started working with chefs and reviewing the data, the trust that consumers place in the industry has hovered between 60 and 70 percent, higher than almost every industry except clean energy.[26]

Even when issues such as health and nutrition are factored in, the industry is still among the most trusted. One study by the Center for Food Integrity ranked restaurants among the most trusted groups when it came to food safety and among the groups that the public held responsible for food safety.[27] Theories abound as to why, but it is most likely because we also have tremendous faith in the food system not making us sick or killing us.

But being both responsible for and a trusted source of food puts chefs and restaurants alongside other credible influencers, including farmers, dieticians, and family doctors.

With this trust also comes a sense of responsibility for chefs such as Reusing. "Once I started getting into the world of advocacy, it became clear that people expected me to have all the information or facts," she explained. "So, I needed to be more prepared and learn more about the issues I was working on such as immigration and farmworker rights. These are areas where others have more lived experience, and I also wanted to be sure I was representing them well. I work very hard to maintain trust with my customers, the policy makers I talk to, and the people I'm working alongside. Nothing is more important."[28]

Natural-Born Storytellers

One of the things I love about chefs is the way they bring to life the stories behind the ingredients on the plate. In a chef's hands, each ingredient tells a story—of its place of origin, its traditional uses, and the people who grew it or prepared it. Bringing these stories forward is also a privilege.

Not everyone feels safe, empowered, or supported to take a public stance on an issue. As a trusted spokesperson, you can help give voice to stories that might otherwise be ignored and help accelerate change on the issues you care about. It all begins with learning to tell your personal story and make a connection to your audience.

I first met chef Elle Simone at South by Southwest in Austin, Texas, and over the years I've grown to know her as an entrepreneur, cookbook author, and culinary personality. She was the first woman of color to host *America's Test Kitchen* and founded the organization SheChef, which supports Black women business owners in the food and hospitality space. She is a celebrity chef.

She is also someone who used public assistance, including food stamps (now SNAP, the federal Supplemental Nutrition Assistance Program), to help her finish culinary school and launch her career. Without public assistance, it is likely that she would have fallen into debt and had to drop out of school. Instead of being ashamed of that time in her life, Simone uses that experience to help others see the other side of the issue and look beyond the stereotypes and tropes that opponents of SNAP use to attack and defund the program.

More than forty-two million people (about twice the population of New York State) in the United States access SNAP benefits,[29] yet lawmakers are inundated with false stories of fraud and abuse by recipients. Many think SNAP recipients are lazy and don't work.

Debunking myths like these is one reason Simone chooses to share her story with the media and policy makers. "There is nothing wrong with the people who use SNAP. They aren't lazy. They just may need a little extra help. I chose to use SNAP. It helped free me of the stress of wondering where food was going to come from. Hunger is debilitating, and SNAP was a way for me to focus on school, focus on working," she said.[30]

Simone's story is compelling when you hear it over coffee, but it is even more powerful when she tells it to policy makers, especially those who believe many of the myths about SNAP recipients. By sharing her story in person, on social media, in interviews, and in one-on-one meetings, Simone also helps ensure that her ideas break through the clutter and stick.

Demand for Chefs to Get Involved

By claiming the role of chef, you are someone who wants to take on a leadership role. It's expected and needed, of you. Leadership is built into the very definition and meaning of *chef*; the root word, which can be traced to Old French, means "head."

You are the head of the team and are in charge of most of the day-to-day decisions in a restaurant, especially around menu design and sourcing. Often, you are also in charge of hiring, training, and mentoring the line cooks, and in many cases, you quickly become the face of the restaurant or kitchen. As you grow your business and personal brand, and profit from the system, you will also cultivate important relationships and be granted access to the highest levels of government. Given all that, you not only deserve a seat at the table, but you have a responsibility to step up and support movements to fix our global food system.

Your words, your actions matter. Yet, especially in divisive times, many chefs wonder if they shouldn't stay out of debates about policy.

The answer is a resounding no—people want you to get involved. A US public opinion study found that two-thirds of the general public (65 percent) expect leaders and chief executive officers to take the lead in affecting social change.[31] The public wants chefs and others involved with the food system to take on a more direct role in helping solve the problems endemic to both the food system and communities around the world.

It hasn't always been this way, with chefs often being told by everyone from customers to the media to "just shut up and cook." The criticism can even come from within the industry. In 2012, the *Wall Street Journal* published a piece by culinary instructor Julie Kelly calling out chef Tom Colicchio for his work on behalf of increased funding for school meals, writing, "So, Tom, with all due respect, please stick to your pots and pans. You have something to offer. If you want to advance the food movement, educate people on how to cook food. Period. And leave the proselytizing to the politicians."[32] (Colicchio responded by cofounding

Food Policy Action, the first organization to create a score-card assessing Congress's support of food policy.)

But it is impossible to dismiss the role chefs play in promoting policy changes and modeling best practices in their own kitchens and businesses. Kevin Concannon, who served as chief of the nation's nutrition programs during the Obama administration, defends chefs, saying, "When chefs weigh in, they are rightly viewed as experts on the importance of food in all of our lives."[33]

Chef Bootcamp and Chef Action Network

When you consider their influence, it's hard to argue that chefs shouldn't have a seat at the table in reforming our food system. I'm grateful, every day, that Kessler and Nischan called bullshit on my concerns and pushed me to join them at that first training and the pilot Chef Bootcamp for Policy and Change. What I learned there led to a decade-plus of working with one of the most generous, innovative, and thoughtful communities of business owners and advocates out there. It hasn't been without complications or without coming face to face with the darkest realities of the restaurant industry, but when trained to use their platforms effectively and generously, chefs can be counted on as powerful champions for much-needed changes and reforms to their own industry—and the greater food system.

I was joined at that first Chef Bootcamp by many of the best chefs in the United States. James Beard Award winners Hugh Acheson, Michael Anthony, Jeremy Bearman, Maria Hines, Andrea Reusing, Cathy Whims, and Alex Young came, as did then-nominees Jeremy Barlow,

Sean Brock, Colby Garrelts, Ed Kenney, and Joseph Lenn. Chefs known for their work on cooking competition reality shows, including *Top Chef*'s Sam Talbot and *Hell's Kitchen* winner Rock Harper, were also among the participants. Held in partnership with the James Beard Foundation and PEW Charitable Trust, the idea was to spend the weekend educating the chefs about the overuse of antibiotics in meat production and inspire them to join a PEW-led campaign called Chefs Against Superbugs.

In addition to their culinary ability, each chef was recruited specifically based on a variety of factors, including the size of their social media following and their public profile. Together they formed a culinary supergroup.

Over three days, we developed the first framework for the education and training program that would be used over the next eight years to train thousands of chefs, farmers, mixologists, owners, and food activists around the United States. That weekend, though, started as a mash-up of tried-and-true advocacy training techniques, scientific briefings, and culinary experiences. What I learned trying to bring these things together for chefs and restaurant owners changed the course of my life. It started me on a journey to join the fight for a stronger, more effective set of tools for those in the industry interested in changing the food system.

Throughout this book, I'll break down the program for you, introduce new tools, and help you adapt them to fit the issues and causes you care about. But in that first training, we were throwing spaghetti at the wall to see how best to help culinary superstars effectively use their voices and platforms in support of a controversial topic: our meat supply. We found that some tools—such as email templates, weekday briefings, and press conferences—just don't fit the life of a chef or restaurateur. Culinary professionals live on social media, text messages, and WhatsApp. We realized that the true chef superpowers were tied to storytelling and networking, skills that almost every person in food comes by naturally.

The chefs that weekend helped us—the professional advocates and trainers—adapt our work to fit their lives and expertise. Together we created training that was, at its heart, by chefs and for chefs and others who earn their living in the real-time world of food production, restaurants, and hospitality.

The chefs discovered that they had the power to drive changes to our food system in a variety of ways by including their own restaurants and operations in such changes, connecting more purposefully with community-based organizations, and amplifying efforts to change public policy at the local, state, and national levels. We learned that we, as trainers, needed to make sure that we could articulate how every policy change was going to affect their lives and operations at each of those levels—the table, the community, and policy. Together we also experienced the harvesting of live animals—a part of the training that wasn't planned but later became a signature of future retreats—and how to take the emotion and education of the experience and incorporate it into our own thinking about food systems and food politics.

At the end of the retreat, after all the discussions and training exercises (including a set of role-playing exercises that helped participants practice talking to members of

Congress), the chefs cooked together. Whenever anyone asks me about the best meals I've had in my life, I answer that it is an unfair question. The meals cooked at the end of each Chef Bootcamp are my overwhelming favorites. That last night, watching the chefs cook together, tasting Whims's tomato pie and Reusing's lamb ribs and experiencing their version of "family meal," it became clear to me that they had the ability to be leaders and advocates.

They knew it, too. They were scared straight by the scientific briefing by Dr. Lance Price, a globally recognized expert on the impact of antibiotics. They better understood that their purchases of animals, particularly beef, from commodity farms were helping perpetuate a system that overstuffed antibiotics into all our bodies and is endangering our health. They understood their role in helping tell the stories of the farmers and ranchers they worked with and how a small (but not simple) regulatory change could help shift the course of antibiotic resistance in the United States. They were inspired and motivated to do more. Before all the chefs left on the last day, they got together and brainstormed the creation of a new coalition—the Chef Action Network (CAN)—and committed to bringing other chefs and restaurateurs into the work.

When they looked at one another to see who would take it forward and no one knew what to do, they looked at me. I was so taken by their energy and expertise that I said I would figure out how to proceed. When they told me they didn't have the money to start, I said I would work for food. There were some chuckles, but honestly, for years CAN was a labor of love, and chefs around the country repaid me with extra items delivered to a table and care packages of Meyer lemons and homemade jams and chocolate.

From 2012 to 2020, I led eighteen Chef Bootcamps for Policy and Change for CAN and the James Beard Foundation. More than three hundred chefs went through the program and joined CAN. Hundreds more joined a waiting list, and as the founding executive director of CAN, I set out to also build a series of local and regional training courses using the same rubric. I traveled from coast to coast to meet and educate chefs about ways they could get involved in some of the biggest fights in food policy from hunger to antibiotics to GMO (genetically modified organism) labeling to food waste.

Over time, CAN hosted days of action in Congress, brought chefs to meet with officials in the White House, and I worked with chefs around the country to publish op-eds, host forums in their restaurants, launch TED Talks, and build their own campaigns and organizations. Every day, I watched and supported chefs as they chose to step into the public eye on issues related to food and restaurants. It wasn't always easy. They didn't always get it right or win the policy fight. What they did was learn, experiment, try, and try again.

A Is for Advocacy

As members of the restaurant industry, you have the raw ingredients to create important change. When I laid this out in the first Chef Bootcamp, chef Maria Hines raised her hand and said, "So our mise en place is ready." Every chef nodded in agreement. But as any good chef knows, ingredients are not enough. You need a recipe and training—a lot of it.

When I was in my twenties, my family built a restaurant in Niceville, where I grew up on the panhandle of Florida. Called the Old Post Office, it sat just off the center of town and, between the lunch crowd and locals celebrating special occasions or just taking a break from cooking at home, served hundreds of people each day. The first time I stepped into that kitchen during dinner service, I was terrified. It was chaotic, loud, and dangerous.

Waiters came in through the swinging door to line up more tickets, and a rundown was given to the line. The executive chef was Italian, but the back of the house staff was mostly Mexican immigrants and white high school students, so the language of the kitchen was a broken mix of made-up terms and hand motions. There were five people working at various stations, and there was a constant call and response: fire two veal; yes, chef; need four more lasagnas; yes, chef; VIP on fifty-one; yes, chef. It continued, unabated, for hours. Then there were the sounds of boiling water, sizzling fat, slicing knives, and clanging pans.

But the longer I stood in the kitchen, in the pass where final dishes and tickets are matched up before a waiter picks them up to bring to a customer, the more I realized it wasn't chaos I was watching but a carefully designed and managed team. Everyone in the kitchen—from the dishwasher to the line cook to the executive chef to the server—was working together. Every person knew their job, every ingredient was prepped, and every dish, glass, and utensil was organized in a way to make every move, and every choice, purposeful, easier, and safer. The level of skill and training needed to run service during a mealtime rush inspires awe and respect.

As a professional chef, you will probably have trained for at least ten years before becoming the one who leads a kitchen and a team of cooks and servers. Some of you may have attended culinary school, and some may have come up working in a kitchen. Regardless of where you got your education, you will have spent thousands of hours to get to a point where your kitchen runs safely and effectively.

This same level of training and attention to detail is essential to learning to champion issues, especially in an increasingly fragmented society. To be a successful advocate—someone who gets other people to support your beliefs—you must figure out a way to bring people into a conversation in a way that inspires them to act.

The different actions we all take, especially now with entrenched social media tools, help raise our friends' and followers' blood pressure. Unfortunately, "likes" don't automatically translate into real-world change. To have a real impact, we all need to better understand how to make arguments, lift up causes and points of view, and claim our seats at the policy-making tables. which are not innate skills for most. You will need to work at it. Thankfully, the challenging work has been done to perfect a framework that you can easily adopt.

Over the last several decades, every winning campaign and movement had similar campaign structures and critical attributes that helped drive their success. As I built out the training program for chefs, I studied and analyzed hundreds of social cause campaigns. From that research, a template appeared to help train people on how to step up and shape practices and policies that improve their lives, environment, and communities. These tools are proven and can work for everyone—local business leaders, celebrities, moms, farmers, and even chefs.

Successful advocacy campaigns, like well-run restaurants, all share some basic DNA. They clearly articulate what they want to achieve, know who they are talking to, tell people what they want them to do, and have a clear and easy-to-understand message. I built the "A Is for Advocacy" framework for the Chef Bootcamp for Policy Change. It is a straightforward way to remember the tools and skills you need to effectively use your voice for change.

The set pieces—audience, argument, allies, ask, action, and attention—make up a simple recipe that you can adapt into your very own. Each helps people—and will help you—think strategically about how to open conversations and start to create the conditions for groups to align their thinking and drive change. You cannot do it alone. It is simply not possible to change the world without involving other people and organizations. That is true of all the steps it takes to get a dish from concept to the customer's plate. It is also true for being a successful advocate. You must plan out a way to bring people into a conversation and motivate them to support you and your approach.

Much like professional athletes, musicians, and artists, chefs train and practice for years. You are creative problem solvers and dynamic decision makers. Nothing phases chefs and restaurant owners. Over the years, I've worked with thousands of chefs on campaigns to reduce food waste, shift their menus to support more environmentally sustainable choices, and carve out new policies and practices to professionalize the industry.

By understanding the power of your celebrity and the potential reach of your voice, you can be more than a person who plays with sharp knives and makes delicious food. You have the potential to be a powerful champion for change in our food system. I hope you'll recognize your mise en place, adopt the "A Is for Advocacy" frame, and join in the fight.

Chef Spotlight: Ashley Christensen and Andrea Reusing

Thousands of chefs took part in the training using "A Is for Advocacy," including hundreds who went through the James Beard Foundation's Chef Bootcamp for Policy and Change. Two of those chefs, Andrea Reusing and Ashley Christensen, used the framework to narrow their efforts and discover ways to have a greater impact.

Christensen, chef-owner of Poole's Diner and AC Restaurants in Raleigh, North Carolina, worked with Share Our Strength's No Kid Hungry for years but believed that she could be helping them in bigger ways. She was also looking for a way to more deeply engage her staff and her large community of chefs in efforts to reduce child hunger. As part of their charitable work, she decided to work exclusively with No Kid Hungry from 2016 to 2019 on food insecurity issues. During that time, each of her restaurants highlighted No Kid Hungry on their menus, and they gathered chefs from around the United States to take part in an annual dinner that, in 2019, raised more than $200,000 to help ensure that more kids have access to free school meals. Going deep on one issue with one organization also opened doors beyond fundraising. Leveraging the credibility she had built up by focusing, Christensen met with members of Congress and her local representatives to push for increased funding for school food and summer meal programs.

Focusing was a win-win for No Kid Hungry and Christensen. "Everyone at our restaurants responded really well, from the staff to our guests. People knew why hunger was so important to us and what we are doing about it," she said.[34]

"It's so important to us to work closely with chefs and owners such as Christensen," said Debbie Shore, cofounder of Share Our Strength. "The relationship is stronger, fundraising goes up, and we have authentic champions who can carry our message to their members of Congress in a meaningful way."[35]

Reusing had a similar experience when she decided to focus in part on immigration and farmworker rights. Reusing is laser-focused on making everyone who harvests the food we eat visible to chefs, their guests, and customers. She visits with everyone from farmers to farmworkers to farm inspectors and learns the policies and issues that control the food system. She also uses her platform to share the stories of the farmworkers and encourages her customers and friends to support local organizations, shop more directly and personally, and recognize that we can all help make a place for the discussion around the rights and conditions for food and farmworkers at our tables.

"We've come to see cheap food as our right. Avocado, grapefruit, and asparagus on demand. Chicken so cheap we can eat it three times a day. All of this only possible because of the near-slavery conditions on farms across the United States. The production of even the most pristine ingredients—from field or dock or slaughterhouse to restaurant or school cafeteria—is nearly always configured to rely on cheap labor, work that is very often performed by people who are themselves poor and hungry," she explained. "Inequality does not affect our food system—our food system is built on inequality and requires it to function. The components of this inequality—racism, lack of access to capital, exploitation, land loss, and nutritional and health disparities in communities of color, to name some—are tightly connected. And we are all part of this system."[36]

Chapter 2

Focus Your Efforts

I really started to understand that we are really built into our communities in a way that no other business is. I felt like I had a role to play and that I could do something. I could serve our industry and be part of a team that was making change in a real way.
—*Sue Bette, owner of Bluebird Hospitality in Vermont*[1]

Chefs and restaurant owners have a powerful role as advocates for a better food system, but getting involved is harder than it looks. It requires education, training, focus, and time—time that many do not have. The life of a chef or culinary professional already comes with long hours, physical exhaustion, and mental stress. It also involves time away from family and friends, and the not nine-to-five hours make it difficult to do even mundane tasks such as going to the dry cleaner. It is a lot to ask that you get directly involved in politics and advocacy—it is not like there is room on the to-do list.

It's also confusing and hard to understand where to start. Our "food system" includes producers, processors, shippers, retailers, food preparers, and consumers. Governments play a vital role in the food system by establishing standards and overseeing their enforcement. Supporting roles are played by trade and consumer organizations that inform policy and by professional organizations and academic institutions that engage in research and education. Consumers—whether individuals or businesses—hold tremendous power, but their decisions are guided by the policies and guardrails put into place before food even hits a shelf or plate.

To make any changes in public policy, advocates must navigate a complex and multilevel system. At least a dozen federal agencies implementing more than thirty-five statutes make up the federal part of the food safety system (which is different than the group of laws related to hunger and feeding programs). Twenty-eight US House of Representatives and Senate committees provide oversight of the statutes regulating the system.[2] This level of complexity is repeated at the state and local levels. In 2019, according to the National Council of State Legislatures, more than seven hundred bills regarding food and food safety were introduced across the United States.[3]

That's a lot to sort through, but there is even more.

To influence policies, at any level, advocates must also compete with thousands of paid lobbyists, advocacy groups, and other advocates. According to a 2019 report by the Center for Responsive Politics, nearly nine hundred organizations lobbied the US Department of Agriculture (USDA) on food and agriculture issues that year.[4]

The Farm Bill is an example of just how complicated the system is. It is the largest food-related bill that comes before Congress, and it takes years to write, negotiate, and pass into law. The bill's thirteen titles set the course of America's food and agriculture policy. In 2018, the bill included $867 billion in funding for everything from food waste reduction pilot programs to crop subsidies and more.[5] It includes all or part of every federal program that impacts US domestic and international food security programs, many of which grow year over year. The critical programs benefit from a system in which more than five hundred groups and companies hired lobbyists to advocate for their interests. Estimates put the lobbying spend at close to a billion dollars, making the Farm Bill the fourth most lobbied bill during the entire 2017–2018 Congress.[6]

It isn't just the Farm Bill, and it's not just the food system. Throughout this book, I highlight some of the systemic and societal ills that exist in every industry, not just food and restaurants. I'm unapologetic in my belief that everyone who works in food can do more to address problems we face—from the destructive impulses of colonialism and capitalism to the violence and oppression in sexism and racism to the continuous extraction from the land and sea. No person can dismantle the broader systems at play alone, but we can all do our part to remake them, first by leading by example and then by influencing others to make changes.

It also means—and this may be uncomfortable for some—that your advocacy work will be seen as political. It is important to understand the difference between political advocacy and partisan politics. This work isn't about being a Democrat, Republican, or Independent. It is about identifying the problems plaguing our food system, solutions to fix them, and the ways you can use your voice to accelerate change.

As an individual advocate, getting involved for the first time probably feels overwhelming. I'm still surprised at how complicated and frustratingly hard it is to change our food system. It is daunting, and there doesn't seem to be a straightforward way to understand the best ways to get involved and help accelerate the changes. So, we start where any chef starts—with passion and a plan.

Break it down—determine the problem you want to solve and build your personal approach and strategy. For most chefs, there are three broad categories to work on: making changes to what is on the plate, addressing industry challenges, and using your voice to support larger policy change at the state and local levels.

Rewriting the Menu

For many people working in restaurants and hospitality, the easiest way to address problems with the food system is by changing what is on the plate and the practices in kitchens and dining rooms. Most people in the food system are most comfortable in the kitchen—and making different decisions about operations, sourcing, and purchasing—but may not see it as direct political action or advocacy. It is.

The restaurant industry is responsible for nearly $2 trillion in direct and indirect contributions to the food economy.[7] This figure is everything from linens and flowers to food purchases to wages and benefits for employees. When redirected toward more sustainable farming methods or women-owned businesses or Black-led cooperatives, chefs and restaurateurs can play a decisive role in creating trends and influencing purchasing across the food chain.

By exercising your financial and purchasing power to support local, organic, or sustainable food (or products produced by women or Black farmers), you are taking part in another form of activism that primarily works to influence behavior and purchasing change.

Chef Michael Cimarusti is an enthusiastic advocate for sustainable seafood and addressing seafood fraud and unfair labor practices in the industry. In 2016, Cimarusti helped create Dock to Dish, one of the first community-supported fishery partnerships in the Los Angeles area.[8] This program allows local fishers to sell directly to local chefs, like land-based community-supported agriculture programs. It is designed to use fishers' stories and products in the area to influence everyone's buying habits, from chefs to customers.

In Cimarusti's view, the program is also a way for customers to join the sustainable seafood movement and for small businesses to influence the whole supply chain and big companies and suppliers. "Once you prove that this is a system that delivers traceable seafood without adding a tremendous cost, people will start to demand it," he said. "People in the larger, more traditional seafood business will start making changes. Once you establish this example, they will want to be part of this whole movement."[9]

Thousands of chefs and restaurant owners share Cimarusti's approach. Chefs interested in showing customers that they support locally grown food may put a Slow Food snail sticker on the menu. Restaurateurs focused on economic fairness may cite their membership in various programs designed to educate chefs about more sustainable sourcing practices, including the Good Food 100 or Slow Food USA programs.

In 2018 and 2019, the Good Food Media Network conducted an industry impact study and found that participating chefs were spending almost 70 percent of their food dollars on "good food" such as wild fish or seafood or sustainably farmed fish or seafood.[10] For Good Food 100 Restaurants founder Sara Brito, such programs demonstrate the economic impact that chefs have when they make different sourcing decisions.

"Purchasing can have an enormous impact. Purchasing is also within the chef's control. In our current political climate, we can all complain about what we need our representatives to do," she said. "But I love the people and organizations emphasizing what is still within our control. It prevents us from sliding into victim mode. If we focus on the things that are in our control, we feel empowered. When we are empowered, we act, and by acting, we see those baby steps. And when we see all the baby steps everyone has made, we see that we have made a real difference," said Brito.[11]

Respecting Culture and Cuisines

Advocating for shifts to purchasing, diet, and ingredients is incredibly important—especially when thinking about the impact our food system has on the environment. It is also an area of advocacy where you should take additional time to learn about a related area of food that has been neglected and deprioritized in food policy discussions: the cultural power of food and how the US government and industrial producers have erased some ingredients and cuisines, which often comes in the form of both colonization and cultural appropriation.

Food is one of the most common forms of cultural appropriation. It essentially happens when a person of privilege (for example, white, financially resourced, connected) elevates a food or cuisine and reaps additional benefits such as financial reward or publicity and fame. Often it comes at the direct expense of people who have been making a similar food or recipe. One of the most egregious examples of such appropriation was a restaurant in Portland, Oregon. The opening of Kooks Burrito was written about widely by Portland's food media, but when the owners admitted to "develop[ing] their menus in part by picking 'the brains of every tortilla lady there [Puerto Nuevo, Mexico] in the worst broken Spanish ever,'" as quoted in an *Eater* article, the restaurant quickly closed.[12] By not paying for the women's time or recipes, the owners had blatantly crossed a line from cultural appreciation to appropriation.

My hope is that if you choose to focus on foods or cuisines that aren't part of your personal heritage, you'll take the time to learn about the history and culture tied to a food and you'll work with (and pay) experts for their time and talent. Unlike other artisans or craftspeople, very few intellectual property protections are available for recipe developers or cooks. It is up to you to ensure that you're not appropriating someone else's work and passing it off as your own.

Colonization is another area that you need to be aware of, especially when advocating for changes to diets or ingredients. Colonization is best understood as a violent act, one that forever changes the life and culture of the people and communities that are colonized. Perhaps the most horrible example is from the 1800s when, as white settlers moved onto the Great Plains, the US government and military systematically set out to eliminate Native food supplies, including pushing the American bison to the brink of extinction.[13] This desecration left tribal communities without food, literally starving them (and their culture) to death. Over the generations, as Native communities were unable to feed themselves in traditional ways, their children and families became increasingly dependent on government food supplies and processed foods. The effects of this campaign to control the food sovereignty of Native Americans persist today. Now, Native Americans account for less than 2 percent of the American population and still suffer from some of the highest rates of food insecurity, poverty, diet-related diseases, and other socioeconomic challenges in the United States.[14]

I saw impacts of this weaponization of our food system up close when I spent time on the Pine Ridge Reservation in South Dakota in the early 2000s. I was working on a US Senate campaign and helping organize voter protection efforts on Native lands. I spent long days driving around the reservation, and I remember being struck that every day, I had to pack my car with water and something to eat because there were so few convenience stores or grocery stores in the area. Many years later, I met Chef Sean Sherman, a member of the Oglala Lakota Sioux tribe, who grew up on Pine Ridge. When I told him about my experience, he firmly reminded me that for the more than forty thousand people who live on the reservation, figuring out where their next meal would come from was part of their daily lives.

He is one of a growing number of chefs around the world using their restaurants as platforms to counter the impacts of both appropriation and colonization. As a cookbook author, James Beard Award winner, and founder of the nonprofit organization NATIFS—the North American Traditional Indigenous Food Systems—he is working to reintroduce products, techniques, and cultures to the dining public in ways that also educate their customers about the systems controlling food choices.

Sherman opened a new restaurant, Owamni, in the spring of 2021 to highlight a decolonized menu. "From the very beginning, we tried to really feature what is regional Indigenous foods," he said. "We cut out colonial ingredients, so we stopped using dairy, wheat flour, cane sugar, beef, pork, chicken, really focused on a lot of wild game, really focused on a lot of heirloom agricultural pieces, a lot of native seeds, working with native farms, lots of wild foods."[15]

For Sherman, it's more than just cooking a delicious meal. "Things like blue corn mush and harmony with chili or wild rice, of course, and getting antelope and bison and rabbits and quails and crickets," he said. "So, there's just a lot of opportunities for us to be really creative with Indigenous foods, and we're just creating a place where that can happen."[16]

He also sees the restaurant as a place to help promote a better understanding of how regional food systems operate. "We need community-based food systems. We need a lot more local, community-based farming. We need better usage of our land. Our work is focused on the culinary aspect and developing a lot of education around that," he explained. "So, we will be using our commercial kitchen as a showcase for utilizing these healthy and regionally produced foods, and doing it for us, in a cultural way—focused on Indigenous cultures of where we are. But anybody can be learning from these systems."[17]

Creating Healthier Kitchens

Changing what we eat is an important form of advocacy, but it is important for chefs and restaurateurs to focus on the human side of the food system. For too long, the restaurant industry—and the greater food system—has limped along with a business model that does not prioritize the health, safety, and well-being of workers. Chefs around the United States are working to shift the economic model—including higher wages, eliminating tipping, addressing equity, and supporting efforts to cut harassment and sexual violence—and prioritizing the health, safety, and economic mobility of their teams.

Improving the mental health of those working in the industry is an area of growing work and advocacy. Mental health is at a crisis point in the industry and in all locations. Clinical depression affects at least 10.3 percent of US food industry workers, and the industry ranks between thirteenth and nineteenth for most suicides by occupation and is second in terms of suicidal ideation, with 5.7 percent of workers reporting they had considered killing themselves within the last year.[18]

The deaths by suicide of two chefs helped catalyze a movement to support workers and start to address the crisis.

In May 2018, chef Noah Zonca took his own life.[19] The conversation about why he killed himself, at first, did not go much beyond the people he knew best—the Sacramento restaurant community and the people he worked the line with every day. Then in June, just a month later, chef and television star Anthony Bourdain took his own life in France.[20]

Bourdain's death by suicide rocked the culinary community, and the tragedy opened a discussion about mental health in the restaurant industry. Hundreds of articles were written about stressors in the industry, including rampant sexual harassment, the physical brutality of the kitchen, and a community that leaned on drugs and alcohol to help them make it through a shift. Many believed that Bourdain's death would help catalyze much-needed reforms in the industry.

There seemed to be interest—and some momentum—in making changes coming out of the tragedies, but the industry's mental health challenges would be harder to tackle. For one, the deaths of Zonca and Bourdain were not isolated. Many did not realize at first that Zonca was only one of at least twelve suicides among Sacramento's restaurant community that year. Furthermore, he and Bourdain were only two of the more than 48,000 suicides in the United States in 2018.[21]

Patrick Mulvaney, owner and chef at Mulvaney's B&L in Sacramento, saw this firsthand, as four of the city's twelve people who died by suicide, including Zonca, worked in his kitchen. He knew that he needed to do something. He needed to act to make sure that everyone in his kitchen knew they had someone to talk to and a way for them to get help.

"It was brutal. Between the middle of December and the middle of January, four people died in Sacramento, hospitality people. Three of them were either working or had worked for us before, and one was a long-time Sacramentan. So, this is about as 'home' as home can get," Mulvaney told *Civil Eats*.[22]

Mulvaney is a quiet, thoughtful person known for his exacting eye when it comes to ingredients and plating. He is a tough and consistent champion for the produce and people in California's Central Valley and, like most chefs, is brief and blunt. He is also a physically large man who normally sports a fresh kitchen wound or two. I was terrified of him the first time we met.

Over years of working with him, it became clear that the heart and passion Mulvaney brings to the kitchen is the same papa bear personality he brings to helping everyone in his community. When he talks about Zonca, the depth of his feeling for this man is evident. Even years later, Mulvaney's voice cracks when he talks about learning of Zonca's suicide, and it is clear that he holds himself accountable for making sure that there are no more Zoncas or Bourdains in Sacramento.

Mulvaney said, "We started to say, as a community, How could we let this happen? How could we let somebody who was so lively and so loved fall apart like that. We started to talk more as restaurateurs and chefs about what our responsibility was. Did we cause this? What's the solution?"[23]

He also knows all the industry's stressors firsthand and thinks the stress is something that attracts certain personalities. "You have to be fucked up to work in restaurants," he said. "There's an acceptance that we're an industry that takes misfits. Combine that with late nights, a play-hard approach, and an alpha culture, and it can be a lot. We needed something in place to help these kids know they have worth beyond what they put on the plate. We needed them to know help was available." Mulvaney concluded that "this is a place for me to help my people. We are storytellers at the end of the day. And one of our stories is going to be about mental health."[24]

Mulvaney was able to take these stories into conversations with the lawmakers, including California governor Gavin Newsom and Representative Doris Matsui (D-CA), regulars at the restaurant, to make a case for explicitly including restaurant workers in the state's landmark mental health funding pool.

"Mrs. Matsui, Doris, has been coming into the restaurant for years, and she's a long-time champion of extending health care to include mental health care. I know it is an important subject to her, and I was able to spend some time talking to her about Noah, about all the others," said Mulvaney. "Because we had a relationship, she listened and supported our efforts. It was the same with the governor. I have particular access to them, and I used it to focus them helping restaurant workers."[25]

As Mulvaney sees it, it is not enough to only help the workers in California. He wants mental health supports to be standard in every restaurant and in every community. "If we can affect even one person, then we're good at my restaurant," he said. "But I want these conversations to happen in kitchens around the country. Talking about our mental health, what we need to survive, should be as easy and normal as running down the daily menu at family meal."[26]

Dismantling Outdated Ways of Operating

Chef Jenny Dorsey is another chef focused on changing the way the industry operates. Using food, culture, and technology, Dorsey founded Studio ATAO (it stands for all together, at once) to create conversations about topics not being addressed in more mainstream fine-dining settings, including social justice, tokenism, exploitation in food media, and racism. In her work, she wants to bring new people into difficult conversations to help drive changes in the industry.

"The hardest part of advocacy and activism is it's hard to engage people who are not already engaged. There are so many people on the fringes, and we're finally starting to have a conversation," she said. "How do we get 'allies' who are at best performative, but at worst upholding white supremacy, into an experience that then can prompt them to not only reconsider and have some introspection, but have an interpersonal connection with someone else? That is a powerful tool to drive change. Being able to establish a space where that can happen and those conversations are prompted is the founding idea for our in-person events."[27]

These events prompted Dorsey and the team at Studio ATAO to research and publish a series of guides and training materials to educate people and encourage them to share what they have learned with others in their circle.

The first tool kit, "Recognizing, Disrupting, and Preventing Tokenization in Food Media," received national media attention and was downloaded by people around the world. They followed it up with a second guide, "Toolkit for Implementing Systematic Changes towards Equitable Representation in Media Companies." Each guide contains useful baseline definitions for terms such as *tokenism*, how it contributes to oppression in the food system, and how tokenization shows up in food media. The guides, available on Studio ATAO's website, also contain practical ways that people can help address the issues, and resources to help. (More information about the work of Studio ATAO and other chef-supported groups featured throughout this book is available in the appendix.)

In addition to addressing racism and exploitation in food media head on, Dorsey and the Studio ATAO team are also exploring ways that the industry can become more antiracist and equitable through cooperative business models, revenue sharing, and the elimination of the subminimum wage for workers and the industry. "We start with conversations with industry professionals about a specific social impact topic that pertains to them. Then we build the tools to change things. We started with food media and had food media professionals come together to talk about tokenism in food media, what it means, how it happens, and how to disrupt it. That formula works. The industry is the problem; we must produce solutions to fix it. We can't wait for others," Dorsey said.[28]

Addressing Inequality in the Industry

I first met Chef Edward Lee when he walked into the James Beard house on West 12th Street in New York City for a listening session in 2017 around sexual harassment in the industry and the MeToo movement. At the time, the industry was reeling from accusations toward dozens of chefs, owners, and hospitality celebrities. About fifty people showed up that day, and, honestly, most of them just sat and listened to presentations. It was hard to get the conversation going. Lee was one of the only ones who stood up and challenged others in the room to use the moment to do better by their employees and customers. I remember thinking how powerful it was for a James Beard Award winner, author, and someone who was frequently on television—again the celebrity chef—to stand up and call his peers out publicly.

Around the same time, Lee and Lindsey Ofcacek founded the Let's Empower Employment (LEE) Initiative to address inequities in the industry. "There are so many awful, ingrained practices in our industry. There is absolutely no excuse not to change them," he said.[29]

Lee and Ofcacek are looking to grow the number of women owners and head chefs in restaurants. A 2022 survey by the National Restaurant Association found that 63 percent of entry-level restaurant workers are women, but only 34 percent of executives are women.[30] The disparity is even more extreme when it comes to compensation and ownership. Of head chefs, fewer than 7 percent are women (and even fewer identify as Black, Asian, or Indigenous), and they earn about one-third less than their male counterparts.[31] In response, Lee and Ofcacek launched a mentor program in Kentucky for women chefs. They match the women with mentors around the United States, and each woman is provided the education and resources to work for a period in their mentor's restaurant.

"Ninety-nine percent of the problems in our industry could be solved with more women in leadership. This helps give these women the opportunity to build their skills and network and then come back and share that information and training here in Kentucky," Ofcacek said.[32]

More personal to both Lee and Ofcacek is the creation of an emergency feeding project in Louisville named for local chef David McAtee. McAtee was shot and killed by the National Guard during a Black Lives Matter protest just months after the murder of Breonna Taylor and days after that of George Floyd.

"David was part of our chef family. He did not have awards or recognition, but he was incredibly important to his community," said Lee. "He fed everyone. He helped those who needed a meal. He was a generous man. He was a chef, and so creating a place where people would have to remember him and his work was important. We called it the McAtee Community Kitchen to honor him and so that, after all the cameras and media were gone, people would have to continue to say his name, too."[33]

Lee and Ofcacek reached out to one of their mentees from Women Chefs of Kentucky, chef Nikkia Rhodes, to oversee the kitchen, and the kitchen turned out thousands of meals for community centers around the city. The feeding project is now a permanent part of the LEE Initiative's programs and has grown into a job-training and education program. Said Lee, "We are in a position to help change this industry, to help our communities heal. That's what we did with the kitchen. Now, we are making it possible for more people to get training and job skills. Hopefully, that will make a difference, too. This industry can do better."[34]

The McAtee Community Kitchen also inspired a series of partnerships to support Black farmers and restaurateurs, including a multiyear partnership with Heinz (best known for ketchup and other condiments). The partnership provides financial grants to Black-owned restaurants along with promotional support and financial and operational resources. It's something Lee and Ofcacek believe will help change the makeup of the restaurant industry, where fewer than 10 percent of owners are Black.

"Black-owned restaurants are critically important to our communities," said Lee. "We saw this as an opportunity to help ensure these businesses thrive. I hope that it also means that more Black chefs, especially women, will move into owning their own businesses. This is the way we can make sure that this industry is more inclusive and better represents those who work in it. When we change who owns restaurants, when employees start to see a path toward ownership, we can change way the whole industry works."[35]

Changing Policy: The Long Game

After working with chefs around the world, I completely understand the pull of some of the "easier" forms of advocacy. You spend every day in the kitchen, so it makes sense that many of you will be comfortable focusing on ingredients or shifting the industry's cultural and operational norms. Changing the way food is sourced, influencing local economies, and addressing the myriad problems facing the industry are critical components of fixing the food system. If we can change the operations and finances of one of the largest economic drivers, other changes will follow.

I'm here to ask you to do more. True systems change requires policy change. When we change laws, public policies, and regulations, we ensure that changes driven by social movements are codified and protected. Doing so takes longer and requires almost constant care and feeding, but results in meaningful and lasting change in our lives.

Chef Michel Nischan, one of the founders of Wholesome Wave and a cofounder of the James Beard Foundation's Chef Bootcamp for Policy and Change, is one chef who believes strongly in the power of policy. He is a champion for food as medicine, believing that if we change the way we eat, we can influence health outcomes ranging from obesity to heart disease and type 1 diabetes.

Nischan has several family members, including two of his sons, who suffer from diet-related diseases, which informs his worldview. As a chef and restaurateur, he changed all the sourcing at his restaurant, Heartbeat, to highlight healthier alternatives and local farmers. But he also realized that the restaurant's impact was limited. "I'd been patting myself on the back for work I was doing at Heartbeat, but then when I learned that there were tens of millions of Americans who couldn't even afford one head of broccoli as a side, I was looking out over all the white tablecloths and not feeling great about myself," he said.[36]

He started working with former USDA undersecretary Gus Schumacher to build a new nonprofit organization, Wholesome Wave, which worked directly on policy solutions to make it easier for families to source fresh fruits and vegetables. From 2007 to 2014, Schumacher and Nischan built relationships on Capitol Hill, worked with First Lady Michelle Obama and others at the White House, and encouraged USDA secretary Tom Vilsack to create the Food Insecurity Nutrition Incentive (FINI) program. Over seven years, Nischan met with hundreds of members of Congress—both Republicans and Democrats—to build awareness and support for FINI. Funding for a pilot program was finally included in the 2014 Farm Bill.

In its first year, FINI-supported programs at farmers' markets resulted in thirty-two million additional servings of fruits and vegetables for households receiving Supplemental Nutrition Assistance Program (SNAP) benefits, and an estimated $14.3 million in economic activity for participating farmers and communities. After more work by Nischan and Wholesome Wave, the FINI program moved from a pilot to a permanent public benefit. In a special move, the program was renamed the Gus Schumacher Nutrition Incentive Program (GusNIP) honoring Wholesome Wave's founder, who died in 2017. Today, the program puts at least $56 million a year in the hands of food-insecure women and families to buy fruits and vegetables.[37]

"Our work exceeded the expectations of what the world thought a chef and a policy pro could do together. But we knew there was no way to get the kind of money we needed from foundations or donors. We needed the government to step in. The only way to do that was to build up support for the idea and keep at it, day after day. It wasn't easy, and it took a while, but it worked," said Nischan.[38]

Nischan is only one of hundreds of chefs around the United States who work directly to change food policy. Chef-restaurateur Sonja Finn, who had spent time in Washington, DC, lobbying for the Farm Bill and SNAP and working with groups such as the Environmental Working Group, ran for city council in Pittsburgh, Pennsylvania. Although she lost that race, her platform was informed by running restaurants and included calls for universal preschool, infrastructure investment, and raising the minimum wage.

Chef-restaurateur Francesca Hong won her race for the Wisconsin State Legislature in 2021. In a column for *Bon Appétit*, she wrote: "It's important that in my new position I uphold the values I learned in restaurants. The policies we are fighting for . . . to build economic agency and security will make the restaurant industry stronger because we are advocating for investment in people. Whether we serve in the public or private spaces, we must look past centering ourselves and instead focus on taking care of one another." She concluded that "this is what I love most about restaurants, even if the system has flaws. I know we can change it for the better through collective care and collective action."[39]

The experience that chefs such as Nischan, Finn, and Hong bring to the world of policy reform is an important perspective valued by even the most seasoned policy makers. In a session featuring chef Tom Colicchio and Representative Chellie Pingree (D-ME) at American University,

Pingree said this about chefs as policy advocates: "They bring the stories of working men and women to life. Our food workers, whether in the restaurant or the field, live the impacts of our food policies. They are important voices that should be at the table."[40]

Focusing Your Efforts

There are many different issues for you to work on, not just in changing what you serve or how you operate your restaurant, but in the world of policy. It is essential that you prioritize the issues and causes you are interested in and clear the space for your advocacy work—it is time-consuming work.

Think about it as you would when you are designing a new dish or menu. You have to decide the goal you are working toward and put the pieces in place to help you achieve it. Finding that kind of clarity in the chaos of your day is hard. To survive in a professional kitchen, you must be able to multitask. Chefs, line cooks, and everyone in a kitchen learn early on to manage a complicated ecosystem of tasks to produce something appealing and delicious, no matter what the day throws at them.

Preparation can go right out the window, however, with a sudden rush of orders or the delay of a daily delivery. As a result, chefs must stay flexible and figure out every day, even dozens of times a day, how to adapt and realign their process to accommodate everything from pandemics to food allergies to a misplaced order from the wholesaler.

The same can be said about everyone who works in the food system, from farmers and fishers to bartenders and restaurant owners. They plan, prepare, adapt, and overcome all day long. The constant need to multitask and manage crises is admirable, but it can also work against a desire to home in on a problem and commit deeply to any one task or cause.

Finding Your Focus Prep List

1. Know what you are already giving.
2. Find the way to say no.
3. Say yes.

---

1. Know what you are already giving. How you spend your time and money should reflect your values, so knowing how you already spend those two valuable assets is the first step in gaining the focus you need.

To help chefs focus their time and attention, I developed a self-audit to help them discover how many causes, campaigns, and initiatives they were being asked to support each year. After reviewing hundreds of requests for donated labor, books, fancy food items, gift certificates, and more, the audits add up to an industry average of more than $50,000 per restaurant in donations each year. The food and hospitality sector is among the most generous in the world, and any fundraising officer for any charity would tell you that a $50,000-a-year donor would be among the most important people to cultivate and steward.

By comparison, a Bank of America survey found that "on average, high net worth donors gave $29,269 to charity in 2017, up by 15 percent from $25,509 in 2015."[41] Thus, chefs and restaurant owners are more charitable than people with a household income of $350,000 or more, all while trying to run businesses that often have the thinnest margins.

The intent is there, but the scattered approach of these donations undercuts the impact.

So why aren't contributions from chefs and restaurants valued more? In part, it is because the $50,000 is not dedicated to one cause or organization. Instead, it is often parceled out to everything from an individual Girl Scout troop to local food festivals to statewide fundraisers to national advocacy organizations. Sometimes there is no rhyme or reason to how the donations are made, which leads to an unhealthy and unsatisfying transactional relationship between chefs and nonprofit organizations.

A simple exercise will help you understand and prioritize your giving.

- *Add it up.* Look at how much you have been giving away, including gift cards, merchandise, foodstuffs (for example, donated meat or seafood), labor costs, unpaid time for recipe development, travel, set up, payments to staff working on the project with you, and promotional prices. It does not have to be a perfect calculation.
- *Name the organization(s).* List the organizations you have worked with over the last twelve to fourteen months. Include anyone who asked for and received the above resources, such as someone on your team, a partner, or an organization holding a fundraiser.
- *Put it in writing.* Put the summary of this audit somewhere so that you will be able to look at it as

a reminder of all the people and organizations that ask for your help.

Using your voice—and financial resources—for the causes you care about should be among the most fulfilling acts you undertake. Once you have a handle on the contributions you have made—both in time and money—you will be able to take additional steps to focus your advocacy work.

2. Say no. Baked into the food industry is hospitality. The industry is built on unfair and discriminatory tipping policies and the constant devaluation of labor costs and personal agency. Working for a customer's satisfaction, tips, and return business has created an unequal balance. That is true of food service and of how chefs and restaurants treat requests for donations and support. No one ever wants to say no, but to be a strong voice for the issues you care about, you must. That will feel uncomfortable, but if you know what causes you are already supporting, know how much time and money you're contributing, and do the challenging work of answering the question about what is essential, you will have the power to say no.

When you learn to say no, you can say yes much more powerfully. Your yes will be supported by your restaurant's total weight, team, and passion to support your work.

Chef Aaron Silverman, owner and chef of Rose's Luxury, Pineapple & Pearls and Little Pearl in Washington, DC, sees global hunger and food insecurity as a solvable problem. When Silverman opened his restaurants, he did not want just to create world-class restaurants; rather, he wanted to have an impact on the world. That started by talking to his team about what causes they cared about and where they believed they could make a difference. To help build awareness and raise money to help address those challenges, Silverman works in direct partnership with the World Food Program. He and his team established this partnership early, even before the restaurants' doors opened.

His email and standard response to requests for donations focus on what he is working on: to address world hunger. In response to an ask from Food Policy Action and Chef Action Network to take part in a fundraising event and congressional lobbying day highlighting the need to increase funding for school lunches alongside fellow chef Tom Colicchio and *Top Chef* producer Padma Lakshmi, Silverman wrote: "We stick with the World Food Program, and that is it. Try to focus our energy on them to have a big impact. I'd love to donate, but unfortunately, it would open us up to too many other people asking, and we really want to focus our donations/resources on our one chosen charity. I hope you can understand.—Aaron." His response clarifies why he is declining an opportunity to help a particular group. The answer does not change either, even when the question comes from a famous peer.

3. Go ahead and say yes. Once you have done the challenging work and started saying no to all the worthwhile and meaningful causes out there, you get to the fun part of saying yes. Saying yes is more than just agreeing to donate your time and talent to a nonprofit or social movement. It is the start of a deeper and more meaningful journey with the community of people who also care about an issue.

Start by asking yourself (and your investors, partners, and entire staff) what makes you happiest and keeps you up at night. Take a few minutes and write down your response to the question, what issues do my team and I care about most?

There is no wrong answer to this question. Advocacy is personal, so it is vital to work on something you and your team are passionate about and will spend time on. People are motivated to become advocates because they care deeply about something. Do not try too hard to push yourself to care about something that doesn't resonate with you and your team.

Like many other chefs, Charleen Badman, owner and chef at FnB in Scottsdale, Arizona, was used to spending weeks of each year cooking at a variety of charity fund-raisers. The James Beard Award–winning chef took the time to figure out the issues that mattered most to her and is now the cofounder of a chef-philanthropy collaborative called the Blue Watermelon Project, which advocates for better school meals in Arizona. The scope of this project includes classroom training for students, working with local and regional farmers and food purveyors to supply food for the meals, and local policy advocacy efforts. The work finds Badman and the other chefs involved working with everyone from other nonprofits, teachers in the schools, school administrators, and elected officials—anyone who is also working to improve the quality of school meals and teach students lifelong kitchen skills.

"I always felt pulled in a million different directions," said Badman. "Once I decided that school meals would be my focus, I could dig into the problem from all sides. We cannot tackle the entire country, but we can have an impact on our own community. We can make a difference—one kid, one school at a time."[42]

Chef Spotlight: Steven Satterfield, Mourad Lahlou, and Tiffany Derry

Every time you leave food half eaten on your plate or throw out unused produce, you waste all the human hours, natural resources, and money that went into producing, processing, packaging, and transporting your food. This practice is a chronic problem: Americans waste more than 40 percent of the food that is produced in the United States.[43]

The volume of food waste also makes it responsible for nearly 10 percent of global greenhouse gas emissions and is a major contributor to climate change.[44] All this food is being wasted while millions of people are food insecure. Restaurants not only contribute to food waste, but the industry is losing billions each year (as much as $165 billion each year).[45]

Although the problem may feel insurmountable, figuring out how to prevent food waste and loss is a solvable problem. For restaurants, where food costs average around 35 percent of the total budget—and sometimes can be much higher—getting a handle on food waste can be good for both the planet and the bottom line.[46]

Chef Steven Satterfield, co-owner of Miller Union in Atlanta, Georgia, is a pioneer in the area of reducing food waste. "When I first read how much food is wasted, I was appalled. I have deep respect for the farmers and producers we buy from, and wasting their efforts feels disrespectful. It also, as a business owner, costs me money, so it feels like a solvable problem. Sure, the more we focus on reducing food waste the better our food costs are, but it also helps the planet and our farmers," said Satterfield. "Reducing food waste is ingrained in how we operate and how we think about dishes. We hold staff trainings to educate our staff on ways to prevent waste. We also build really delicious dishes, so customers aren't thinking they are eating waste."[47]

For Satterfield and other chefs, preventing waste in the restaurants is just the first step in the education process. Satterfield was one of more than one hundred chefs who participated in the creation of a consumer-facing cookbook and culinary education series developed by the James Beard Foundation (with support from the Rockefeller Foundation). It was clear to Satterfield and other chefs that they could do more than make delicious food—that their voices, as business owners, were useful as lawmakers considered new policies to reduce food waste.

"The more I learned about food waste, the more urgency I felt to do more. The more we tried to do, the more we encountered barriers to making changes in our restaurant, especially in the area of garbage and waste," said Satterfield. "No one wants to talk about waste at the dinner table, but we could only get so far in using every part of the chicken or juicing kale stems. We need changes in policies to make sure that nothing gets wasted. This is true in my restaurant. It's also true for people trying to reduce waste in their homes."[48]

Experts believe that one way to reduce food waste, especially at a consumer level, is to standardize date labels on food, including meat, dairy, and canned goods, and thus eliminate the confusion caused by state-by-state labeling and standards.

Chef Mourad Lahlou, owner of Mourad in San Francisco, found the myriad laws governing food waste confusing. "We watch what we throw away. We try to use everything from the skin of the fish to the bones, from the head to the peel of the carrot. So, it was crazy to learn that there are no national standards for sell-by dates for things such as milk," he said. "We are telling people to throw away food that might otherwise be okay. And it is different in every state. When I learned that, I told everyone I could that we needed to do something. I went to Washington, DC, to try and convince Congress we need commonsense laws to help reduce waste. It makes sense of us as chefs. It makes sense to our customers. But the laws didn't make much sense, to me."[49]

Satterfield and Lahlou were joined in their policy advocacy by dozens of chefs, including Tiffany Derry, owner of Roots Southern Table in Dallas, Texas. Over several months in 2016, Satterfield, Lahlou, Derry, and others met with staff in more than sixty individual congressional offices and with US Senators Debbie Stabenow and Ted Cruz and House members Nancy Pelosi and Beto O'Rourke. These meetings encouraged supporting federal laws discouraging waste, specifically the "best buy" and "use by" regulations.

In these meetings, the chefs shared their personal stories and encouraged the adoption of smart food waste reduction policies. Later that year, USDA released new guidelines to encourage manufacturers to adopt one standard for a "best buy" date to help eliminate consumer confusion.

This policy win helped create momentum for food waste reduction, and chefs, including Derry, continued to visit members of Congress. Together they helped secure the first-ever funding—more than $25 million—for food waste reduction programs in the 2018 Farm Bill.

Derry also worked to raise awareness with consumers about how they could reduce waste in their own homes. She continues to work with organizations such as the National Resource Defense Council's Food Matters program, which has helped create food waste programs in more than thirty cities—and at least eight states now have laws focused keeping food waste out of landfills and cutting down on greenhouse gas emissions.

"As a chef, I was taught not to waste any food—to use everything. I was surprised to learn the extent of the problem, especially given it's a solvable problem," Derry said. "Working on this issue has let me honor our farmers and the demanding work of everyone in the food system. Plus, I've found that my elected officials don't like waste any more than I do. We made it easy for them to understand the problem, and we asked for very specific things. So together, we're making real progress—in my restaurant, at home, and in my community."[50]

Chapter 3

Know Your Audience and Arguments

When I built my restaurant, I was very intentional
about what I was trying to say on the plate. I knew
that I wanted my guests to walk away not just
knowing a lot about the farmers but also how they
could help. It's the same with policy. It all starts with
figuring out who can help you achieve your
goals and then helping them to join you
in doing the right thing.
—*Chef Maria Hines*[1]

One of my favorite things about chefs is your
ability to talk passionately about the causes you care
about, in simple and powerful ways. It comes from your
constant translation of ingredients into a cohesive dish or
menu. The same is true of almost everyone who works in
the food and hospitality industry. From farmers to mixologists to restaurant owners to fishers, the industry is

filled with people who make it easy to understand—and enjoy—complex concepts and flavors.

Food and hospitality professionals are also especially good at tailoring their work for particular sets of customers or audiences. Think of all that goes into designing a menu or restaurant concept. No one place, maybe except for an old-school diner, can satisfy every craving. Instead, you spend hours deciding on what type of food or drinks you want to be known for and then more time deciding on everything from the linens to flowers to tables to music.

Each of those decisions reflects your vision of the customer you're trying to attract and what you want them to remember when they leave the table. You spend time building customer profiles, figuring out the perfect price point for the neighborhood, and creating narratives around your concept. All this work also helps you differentiate yourself from the dozens of businesses in your city and the thousands nationwide.

You must do the same thing when you take on issues outside your restaurants. Whether you want to promote seafood sustainability, reduce child hunger, or support wage increases across the industry, your first decisions as an advocate are to pick your audience and develop the best argument to convince them to support you.

Once, while walking the halls of the Capitol and meeting with members of Congress about school lunch regulations, a celebrity chef looked at me and asked, why is this so hard? After all, it's only common sense to want to make sure kids eat more fruits and vegetables. Unfortunately, common sense isn't always the deciding factor in advocacy. Creating change takes time and strategy. It requires identifying who is in control and tailoring your message specifically to that person or group. It also means knowing who has the power to stop you and prevent change from happening.

In politics and policy, power is often held by companies with the time and financial resources to relentlessly lobby elected officials. Our food system is currently controlled by a small number of companies. Oxfam, a global non-profit organization focused on fighting poverty and injustice, found that just ten companies, including Coca-Cola, Mars, and Danone, control most of the food and beverage options available to consumers through both grocery stores and restaurants. (If you serve San Pellegrino or Perrier in your restaurant, you are contributing to the bottom line of one of the big ten, Nestlé.)[2]

These companies and related industry groups fund studies, donate money to political campaigns, and spend time building personal relationships with policy makers and their staffs. They are also expert at deciding who the decision maker is, telling a compelling story, and making the case for their policy priorities.

You need to learn to do the same thing. The only way to combat billions of corporate dollars in advertising and political contributions is with a powerful wave of voices from within the communities most impacted. Becoming one of those voices can feel uncomfortable, even calculating or manipulative, especially when it comes to causes you care about. But there is nothing wrong with looking at your cause from a new perspective or learning to tell your personal story in a way that helps people see for themselves the benefits of supporting you. Everyone should want kids to have access to a healthy school lunch, but if a politician thinks that it is too expensive or unnecessary, it doesn't hurt to point out that improving school lunches can help grow the local economy and can improve test scores.[3]

And here's where the "A Is for Advocacy" (see chapter 1) framework comes in handy. In this chapter, we're going to dig into the first two A's—audience and argument. We will begin building the tools and strategies you will use to center your audience and create messages and narratives that inspire them to support you and your work.

Know Your Audience

Throughout this book, I will keep coming back to policy change—one of the hardest areas of advocacy—because it is how we codify lasting change. To change policy, we need to work with two primary advocacy audiences, decision makers and influencers. A decision maker is the individual or group who can enact the change you seek. In the world of policy advocacy, the decision maker is usually the elected officials who have the final say on a policy change, so you'll work with them and their staff. The final decision maker could be a mayor, governor, member of Congress, or even the president.

Other people also influence the process. Members of media, lobbyists, professional associations, community leaders, social media followers, and many other people and organizations influence elected officials. (We'll dig into the world of networks in chapter 4.)

A common question I get from folks is, why do I have to pick one audience? There is a belief that there is such a thing as the general public. My answer: there is no such thing. The general public doesn't exist. In the same way that your restaurant or culinary style speaks to specific cultures and communities, you need to make some decisions related to the audiences you're trying to reach.

Although you can share your passions with multiple audiences or try to make your case as broadly as possible, to be successful, you need to prioritize. Not everyone will agree with you or help you, so you need to decide where to focus your time and energy. After deciding which issues you will advocate for, you must decide whom you are trying to recruit to your side. You have to identify the specific audiences you're trying to reach.

Every nonprofit organization, political campaign, and purpose-driven brand makes the same decision. It picks a primary audience (and secondary audiences, too). Deciding who your audience is and understanding what your audience needs (and where your audience gets their information) are critical steps in designing any advocacy campaign or effort.

These steps are especially important when you're working on policy change. There are 535 members of Congress and 50 state governors, as well as thousands of state and local officials. Then there are the thousands of staffers and millions of voters who influence elected officials. Every one of these people is an individual with unique experiences and viewpoints. Your job—our job—is to make sure that we're clear about who we're trying to reach and what exactly we want them to do with the information we're giving them.

When we walked the halls of the US Capitol speaking with members of Congress about the quality of school

lunch, we looked at listings of which members had juris-
diction or control over school lunch. They included members of the House and Senate Agriculture Committees. We
also met with members on the House and Senate Budget
and Appropriations Committees, where decisions about
the funding of government programs are regularly made.
Meeting with those members who have oversight and fund
the program helped us narrow our audiences to those who
understood the program.

If you can narrow your scope, you will be more effective
and powerful. I keep a quote from Dr. Wade W. Nobles
on my bulletin board at home and use it to remind myself
about the power in making the tough choices around audiences. Nobles is the cofounder and past executive director
of the Institute for the Advanced Study of Black Family
Life and Culture, and he defined power as "the ability to
define reality and to have others respond to your definition
as if it were their own."[4]

You want your audiences to pay attention, care, and act
with the same intensity you're bringing. That's how you can
shift power and create change.

Policy Makers Are People, Too

It's natural to want to avoid dealing with elected
officials—most people don't trust politicians or the larger
system of government. Since 1974, the Gallup organization
has tracked the public approval rate of Congress. Rarely
does the approval rate rise above 50 percent. In fact, the
average approval rate from 1974 to 2009 was 39 percent,
meaning that more than 60 percent of the American voting

population didn't feel like Congress was doing its job. The average has gone even lower since then, and in 2021, fewer than 20 percent of Americans approved of Congress's job performance.[5] Many perceive that members of Congress don't serve the greater good—or even respond to the basic needs of the people who elected them. This distrust can seep into advocacy efforts and color our interactions with elected officials.

Like it or not, politicians have tremendous power over our food system, so if you want to change that system, you can't completely avoid elected officials. It helps to not think of politicians as a monolith, but instead to identify the specific people who are potential allies. First, consider the practical question of which government body oversees your issue. For example, if you want to influence the national Farm Bill, it's good to know who's on the Senate and House Agriculture Committees. Then, familiarize yourself with the policy positions and voting records of those individuals.

When trying to sway public officials—or any decision maker—it is critical to understand their motivation and interests. It isn't about you or even the cause you care about; it is all about the person (or people) you are trying to reach. It helps to think through the primary factors that influence politicians' decisions: ideology, information sources, and (re)election.

- **Ideology.** Does your cause fit the official's own philosophy or political ideology? Do like-minded colleagues support it? Does the issue align or separate the official from their political party? Chefs will often tell me that politicians should listen to them because those officials work for their constituents, which is partially true. The hard reality is politicians tend to represent the constituents, voters, and donors in *their own political party* because that's where they get their support. It is important to understand the party's views on the issues that are of interest to you. Although some people will work across party lines, it is increasingly rare, so understand where you are starting in the conversation.

- **Information sources.** Does your cause fit the facts, as the politician knows them? Is it something that matches their personal experience? Politicians and staff get information from many sources, from think tanks and lobbyists to specific news sites. When starting out in advocacy, it's important to make sure you understand where officials get their information, including the organizations and studies they rely on to develop policies. Often, members of Congress and staff depend on partisan resources. For example, Democrat elected officials will often use reports from organizations like the Center for American Progress or, in areas of food policy, the Food Research and Action Center. Republican members may get information from organizations like the Heritage Foundation or the Brookings Institution. It's important to know which information members will trust or think are "fake news."

- **Reelection.** Will your cause support the health or economic security of the politician's district? Ultimately, elected officials must answer to the voters who elected them—and who they hope will reelect

them. You'll have more credibility with your elected
officials if you can show that you have a direct tie
to the area they represent. Also, make sure that you
can show a direct tie to the community's health,
safety, or economic condition; these issues are
always among the top concerns tracked by politicians and their staffs.

Thinking about each of these things will help you address
one of the biggest X factors in advocacy: how will your issue
influence the public's perception of them and their work.

There is deep skepticism about politicians and their
motivations. A large number of Americans view "elected
officials as out of touch, self-interested, dishonest and self-
ish."[6] At the same time, generations of political science
research show that people generally respect and trust the
elected officials in their own community (and congressional district) as long these leaders demonstrate that they are
aligned with us on issues we care about and share common
characteristics (for example, party affiliation or personal
identity) or even geographic background. When we share
similar experiences, research consistently shows that voters
generally find elected officials and candidates more trust-
worthy and relatable.

It is also useful to understand how a politician perceives
themselves and the image they want to convey. Just like
chefs have styles, so do elected officials. Some consider
themselves mavericks and are willing to break all the rules.
Some are more traditional and want to play it safe when
it comes to legislating. Making sure what you're asking of
them fits how they want to be seen—say an empathetic

leader or a champion for change—may help you get a foot in door. Just remember that politicians are people, too. Yes, they have to worry about getting reelected and staying on the right side of donors, but they also have personal opinions and interests, just like you. It's your job to learn what motivates them. Figuring out what ideas and arguments could resonate will help you create openings for conversation and set you up for success.

Unexpected Allies

If chef Joy Crump had made a list of potential political allies for her work on hunger, she wouldn't necessarily have put Representative Rob Whitman (R-VA) at the top. Crump, co-owner of two restaurants in Fredericksburg, Virginia, works extensively with local farms, community gardens, and organizations to help feed nearby families. According to the national advocacy group Feeding America, Fredericksburg is home to nearly thirty thousand people, including more than eleven thousand food-insecure children.[7] Crump sees the need all around her and supports more funding for hunger relief programs.

Looking at her reservation books one day, she realized that her congressman and his staff were regular customers. Whitman, a fiscally conservative Republican, repeatedly voted against funding for food-insecure families, but Crump took on the challenge. When he visited her restaurant one day, she approached his table, and after he complimented her food, she invited him to tour the local farm and community center. She wanted him to meet both the people who grew the vegetables and the families that depended on them.

"I just wanted to make the connection. Hard-working people depend on these programs. My hope was that if we took it into the field, and out of the office, he would see that there was more we could all be doing," said Crump.[8]

Whitman accepted her initial invitation. The two opened a dialogue around the Farm Bill's SNAP program that lasted for several years during the negotiation of the 2018 Farm Bill. SNAP is often described as the "first line of defense" against hunger, serving more than forty-two million Americans each year.[9] Restaurant servers are almost twice as likely than the general population to need SNAP benefits, according to research from Food Chain Workers Alliance and Restaurant Opportunity Center United.[10]

Getting Whitman to support the program wasn't easy, but Crump humanized its impact. "We were trying to show him how programs like SNAP are such an important part of our industry," Crump said. "It was amazing—he was very connected to the stories. At first, the ask wasn't for a specific vote. It was just building a story and opening a dialogue. That was just more realistic with a Republican administration. He wasn't going to do anything rash or buck the party. We needed to show him the human side and connect him back to his roots in agriculture."[11]

To organize her thoughts, Crump used a simple technique I often recommend to chef advocates: she created a basic chart with her goal and the name of the decision maker and then populated it with notes about his personal beliefs and interests, knowledge of the issue, and the benefits to his constituents of supporting her cause.

In her discussions with Whitman and his office, she learned that his personal beliefs about SNAP included the false understanding that the program is rife with financial abuse and fraud. Crump also listened to him express support for a limited role of government. She was able to share with him nonpartisan information showing that SNAP is one of the most efficient government programs and has one of the lowest rates of fraud of any government program. To address Whitman's questions about whether the program was necessary for people in his congressional district, Crump introduced him to constituents who used SNAP and other advocates from around the community.

Building Relationships Pays Off

Policy advocacy takes time. The 2018 Farm Bill took more than two years to negotiate. During that process, Crump met with Whitman several times. It helped that the congressman and his staff were regulars at Crump's restaurants and were thus able to build on their conversations with Crump to create a mutual relationship.

Identifying the right audience and developing a message that resonates were critical to the success of another advocacy effort, the fight for the Restaurant Relief Fund that took place during the COVID-19 pandemic.

I will always remember where I was on March 9, 2020. It was the day I first received calls from worried restaurant owners about whether they should shut down their restaurants over health concerns related to the spread of the infectious coronavirus. They were concerned about their staffs and customers. Wholesale panic hit about the industry's economic survival in mid-March when Cincinnati,

Chicago, New York, Los Angeles, and Washington, DC, shut down indoor dining for all restaurants (and almost every major city quickly followed).

Soon, informal groups sprung up in almost every city and met regularly over conference calls and Zoom meetings to discuss ways to make their case to Congress that the restaurant industry, like banks and airlines, was going to need help to survive. Between March 9 and March 19, led by *Top Chef* judge Tom Colicchio and former White House chef and food policy director Sam Kass, dozens of chefs, including Gregory Gourdet, Kwame Onwuachi, Naomi Pomeroy, Steven Satterfield, and Ashley Christensen, came together to form the Independent Restaurant Coalition (IRC). These leaders leveraged the power of their personal stories and set out to convince members of Congress and their staffs that the industry needed (and deserved) to survive the pandemic. Without immediate financial aid and support, industry leaders warned of an extinction-level event among independent restaurants.

Using a simple Google spreadsheet, the chefs mapped their relationships to all 535 members of Congress and members of the Trump administration overseeing relief efforts. They looked for chefs and restaurant owners in each congressional district and organized phone calls, emails, and video conferences with hundreds of legislative aides. They understood that they had contacts and networks to help them reach members of Congress and their staffs—the decision makers who could vote to supply the industry with direct government aid.

By June 2020, Representative Earl Blumenauer (D-OR) and Senator Roger Wicker (R-MS) had written the

RESTAURANTS Act, which called for a $120 billion dedicated fund for the country's restaurants.[12] Support for the bill grew to more than two hundred bipartisan cosponsors in the House, including Majority Whip James Clyburn (D-SC), Assistant Speaker Ben Ray Luján, Democratic Caucus Chairman Hakeem Jeffries, and eighteen House committee chairs. In the Senate, the legislation was supported by forty bipartisan members, including Minority Leader Charles Schumer (D-NY). Both House Speaker Nancy Pelosi (D-CA) and Treasury Secretary Steven Mnuchin highlighted the legislation as a critical part of any COVID-19 relief package.

On February 27, 2021, more than four dozen chefs and restaurant owners gathered via Zoom to watch the House of Representatives vote on President Joseph Biden's American Rescue Plan of 2021. Many of the people on video conference—including *Top Chef* judges and alums, James Beard Award–winning restaurateurs, owners of small city–based eateries, and chefs and owners with businesses around the country—had been gathering several times a day for almost a year to fight for the very survival of the restaurant industry.

As the final vote tally was announced—a narrow 219–212 victory—people on the call burst into applause, cheers, and more than a few excited expletives. The bill supplied financial relief that would change lives and save businesses, including a new $26.8 billion grant program specifically written to help the restaurant and hospitality industry.[13] While it wasn't the dollar amount that the IRC's leaders had asked for, the unprecedented funding would help thousands of restaurants start to recover.

That alone was enough reason to celebrate, but it was bigger than that. None of this funding would have been possible without the work of the assembled chefs-turned-activists. Yes, the bill would help them, but the bill wouldn't have been likely without them. The fund—sent to the president's desk after action in the Senate and a second vote in the House—was the culmination of almost twelve months of direct advocacy and organizing by the IRC and thousands of freshly minted advocates from the food-and-beverage industry.

Caroline Styne, owner of AOC Restaurant Group and a founding member of the IRC, told the *New York Times*, "I never knew our voices mattered. But we are business owners. Members of Congress and their staff are our customers. When we talk in one voice, with one message, we can make a difference."[14]

Focus on Common Aspirations and Messages

The IRC chefs were successful because they were speaking to the right audience: members of Congress. But they also had the right message. Their arguments were simple, emotional, and directly addressed the economic power of restaurants. The chefs contended that the industry was too important to local communities to be left to fail. Part of their strategy was to highlight the importance of the industry through the personal stories of the owners, workers, suppliers, and customers.

Like the IRC, you need to build an effective argument and create a compelling narrative around why your cause or campaign matters. This second A—the argument—is one area where I've seen chefs really excel (and, frankly, screw up). You are powerful, natural storytellers, and the sharing of personal stories is one of the most powerful forms of advocacy there is today. It helps open conversation and connects us to other human beings.

Stories aren't enough, though. Our most heartfelt experiences will fall flat unless they are coupled with solutions and shared in ways that will inspire others to join us.

For help in developing compelling stories to use in advocacy efforts, I use the Aspirational Communication Model built by Douglas Hattaway. I worked with him when he was refining his approach to helping foundations and leaders become better advocates. He created the model by drawing from research by brain scientists, social psychologists, and consumer marketing specialists. I had the opportunity to work with the model on several projects, including training land rights advocates in Nigeria for the Ford Foundation, and I've continued to share it with almost every group I've trained since then.

Aspirational messaging prioritizes the audience; you craft your messages in a way that helps your audience see themselves in your story. As I learned it from Hattaway, "Our aspirations are our ideas about the kind of people we want to be and the kind of world we want to live in. Social and motivational psychology show that aspirations are powerful drivers of decision-making and behavior. And we're more likely to pay attention to messages that reflect our goals and values."[15] Your goals become their goals. Your common aspirations become the starting point for the conversation, which allows you to define the problems you both face in reaching your shared goal. When you've identified the problem, you can then posit solutions and call your audience into the work needed to achieve your shared goals.

To help people better understand the aspirational framing and how it helps create convincing arguments, I start every narrative training with the question, who wants to end hunger in America? Every person in the room raises their hand. Hands go up—no one wants people to starve.

Then, I ask people to leave their hand in the air if they agree with a series of statements, including "Food is a universal right," "We should provide free meals for every child," and "We should tax people more to pay for school lunches." As the questions get more specific about current policies, fewer people agree with each one and hands fall until, usually, I'm the only person with my hand raised.

My point isn't to embarrass anyone or call them out, but rather to illustrate that we all tend to agree when we start with our hopes and aspirations. No one should go hungry, but we may disagree with how we achieve that goal. Good advocates figure out a way to keep the goal—the common aspiration—front and center in our conversations.

Also, although we may all share a common goal, we don't all have the same interests or way of relating to an issue. If you like science or data, you may respond to studies. If you're focused on personal connections, you may be interested in how an issue affects your friends or family. We all have different things that engage us, so it is important to understand your audience's interests and tailor the types of information you present. When you consider each level of the Aspirational Communication Model, you will be able to develop different angles to appeal to people with different motivations and interests.

In addition to our aspirations, messaging tends to focus on three areas: functional, emotional, and social.[16] Each is important, but depending on your audience, you may lean into one more than the others. (I admit that this advice may sound like a grandmother's biscuit recipe—add flour but not too much, knead for a bit but not too long—but like that recipe, this one will work if you practice it.)

One Fact Is All You Need

Functional messaging is all about the facts. It appeals to our heads, not necessarily our hearts. Many people like to start here, but if you and your audience don't share the same worldview, you may also not share the same understanding of the facts. Remember that we are always motivated to defend our own beliefs, even when they conflict with evidence that is objectively true. So debating facts first is generally not a good idea.

Even if you're generally on the same page with your audience, you want to avoid information overload. Too many facts can leave your audience confused and unable to act on the information you're sharing. Pick one or two facts to help your audience understand why they should care about the problem and focus on the most important thing you want them to remember. John Medina, author of *Brain Rules*, wrote that "the typical human brain can hold about seven pieces of new information for less than thirty seconds. If something does not happen in that short stretch of time, the information becomes lost. If you want to extend the thirty seconds to, say, a few minutes, or even an hour or two, you need to consistently re-expose yourself to the information."[17]

Medina recommends that we share information sparingly, strategically, and in ways that engage our audiences. "Repetition cycles add information to our knowledge base," he wrote. "The timing of repetitions is another key component."[18] Similarly, more than one hundred years ago, German researcher Hermann Ebbinghaus showed that "repeated exposure to information in spaced intervals provides the most powerful way to fix memory in the brain."[19]

We don't want to include too much information or conflicting studies and facts in our messages. Rather, we want our audience to be able to repeat the facts we're sharing, and to do that, they must understand them.

For example, when Crump spoke to Whitman, she always made a point of talking about the more than eleven thousand food insecure children in Fredericksburg. She wanted the congressman to know how many kids would be affected by any policy changes. Likewise, the chefs who lobbied with the IRC repeatedly spoke to members of Congress about the eleven million jobs that were at risk if restaurants didn't receive financial support from the government during the pandemic. In both cases, chef-advocates focused on making sure that policy makers left every conversation with just one fact or data point, not twenty.

Emotions Motivate People to Act

That one fact you focus on isn't enough to keep people involved over the long term, however. You also need to appeal to their emotions. Ask yourself, how do you want your audience to feel? Are you trying to enrage them, inspire sadness or regret, or fill them with hope and possibility? The words (and imagery) we use will combine to shape the level of energy and commitment our audience brings to the discussion. When you're engaging your audience, you're building a relationship with them, and emotional appeals will help strengthen your bond.

This use of emotional rhetoric dates all the way back to Aristotle, who identified three layers of emotional appeal: ethos, pathos, and logos. Simply put, ethos is where you build trust and credibility with your audience. Often, it comes from helping them see you as an expert or trusted source of information. The next layer, pathos, is where you create a sense of empathy and urgency within your audience (and inspire them to act). Then there is logos, where you connect dots and make your audience understand how things impact them (and why they should care). You don't have to trigger all three areas—trust, empathy, and impact—every time, but when you're creating emotional messages, keep them in mind. It will help you be more persuasive.

This strategy worked for the IRC chefs where, when talking to members of Congress, the chefs and business owners not only talked about the number of jobs at risk but also the special role that restaurants play in every community. In a series of interviews and columns placed by the coalition, chefs repeatedly invoked the power of restaurants using messages created by the IRC:

> Local restaurants are an impactful gathering place for communities, where relationships form and memories are made. They preserve agriculture and recipes from

generation to generation and are the lifeblood of regional food culture. When you choose to dine at a local restaurant, you invest your money right back into the hands of your community and preserve local recipes and agriculture.[20]

Chef Cheetie Kumar, a member of the IRC's advisory board, testified before Congress about the power of restaurants, saying:

I am proud to be here representing the hundreds of thousands of independent restaurants across the country and their millions of employees. My story is not very different from so many others in the restaurant industry. With my family, I immigrated from India to the Bronx at the age of 8 and eventually settled in the South to play music and open my restaurant. Our industry is full of these stories—from folks all across the country and all around the globe. Women, minorities, single parents, veterans, and so many others get their start in restaurants, build their lives working in restaurants, or make a career out of working in restaurants. Frankly, restaurants represent America more than any other industry.[21]

The imagery of restaurants in every community, made up of people from every part of the United States supporting local businesses, created an emotional, motivating picture for members of Congress, a majority of whom supported the IRC's call for industry-specific relief during the pandemic.

Joining In or Standing Apart

Emotional appeals often work best when paired with a social message. A basic truth is that most people want to belong to a group. As laid out in Abraham Maslow's hierarchy of needs theory, humans crave love, belonging, and acceptance. Our need for those things drives many of our actions, including our engagement in advocacy. Connecting to like-minded people through political, religious, and community groups can both support social change and foster a sense of personal identity and belonging.

By helping your audience identify personally with the issue you're working on, you should be able to maintain the conversation and grow your relationship. You may not win them over at once, but when they see themselves in the community focused on solutions, they will be more open and receptive to discussions and different points of view. In our work as advocates, we are trying to break down outdated systems of control, including othering. Typically, those with the most power in our society—the media and government officials—shape the system, including our perceptions of others, as well as social and cultural norms, creating a world where we only see "others" and a dynamic that is very much "us versus them." When you create opportunities for sharing and dialogue, you can create openings for change.

That's how Crump was able to open a dialogue with Whitman. She didn't attack him or try to shame him into doing things her way. Instead, she started a conversation that went on for years. It is also how the IRC was successful in gaining support from hundreds of members of

Congress. Chefs approached each conversation to draw people in and make them part of the solution.

Using the aspirational frame, successful advocates create what is called thoughtful messaging. According to the Principles of Social Psychology, a resource that includes concepts and practices, which Hattaway and others have adapted to fit the work of policy advocacy, "Thoughtful message processing occurs when we think about how the message relates to our own beliefs and goals."[22] By helping your audience identify personally with the issue you're working on, you should be able to maintain the conversation and grow your relationship with them. Once you've attached your causes to your audience's hopes and dreams, you can also pinpoint how they want to show up in conversation.

Maslow's theory posited that we are motivated to take actions that make us feel safe, secure, and accepted and to achieve esteem from others and self-respect. As Maslow put it, we also want to connect to others and strive for "self-transcendence."[23] As humans, we ultimately want to be part of something and connect to larger causes and communities. Our job as advocates is to help each other look beyond divisive rhetoric and partisanship to recognize what we have in common and what brings us into community with one another instead of separating us.

In the House of Representatives, Blumenauer was initially skeptical of the IRC's efforts to win restaurant-specific relief in 2020, but he ultimately became one of the industry's strongest supporters. When aid passed, he said, "This is a major step forward in the fight to save the local restaurants that make our communities whole. It's been about one year since I first gathered with the Portland restaurant community to come up with a plan to bring relief to beloved dining and drinking establishments and protect the jobs, supply chains, and local economies they support. What started as a local effort to save local restaurants became a national movement that secured $28.6 billion in relief funds that will be available soon."[24]

Building Trust Matters

One of my favorite things about using the aspirational message is that when we build trust, share our stories, and help people see their place in solving the problems in front of us, we also build relationships that last and that help us achieve other goals. Advocates have used arguments and messaging that play on our fears and create unnecessary divisions for too long. It's a strategy that, unfortunately, has worked really well and, in my opinion, has contributed to an increasingly polarized world. It's also something that I see in the food world: everyone has an opinion about food. Too often, instead of saying that something isn't to our taste, we'll say that it's gross, which diminishes the time, talent, and heritage it honors. We dismiss other people's personal tastes or preferences based on everything from where they live to what they wear when they walk into a restaurant.

Using the aspirational frame also helps us break through judgment and negativity. It helps create trust and amplifies shared goals. Aspirational messaging works because you won't have to coerce or strong-arm someone into supporting you. Instead, you'll open up conversations and help find common ground.

The IRC chefs did that over the course of more than two years of direct conversations with policy makers. They coupled the personal stories with data about the industry and the dire economic consequences if it was left to fail. The messages used by the coalition were simple, factual, emotional, and aspirational and helped them secure the funding they needed. Here's a sample from chef and restaurant owner Paul C. Reilly in Colorado:

> You may not realize it, but we all have five favorite restaurants. Five places that you frequent—be it once a week, once a month, or a couple of times a year. You probably consider yourself a "regular" at these spots. . . . Now, imagine a world without that favorite restaurant—or any of your go-to spots. No place to grab a quick drink and a chat. No place to celebrate a happy occasion. No place to gather and make memories around a table. This notion of life without restaurants is a stark reality now thanks to the COVID-19 crisis.
>
> On a national level, restaurants are an essential piece of our economy and without them—without us, the hospitality industry—a recession is imminent. Besides providing essential sales tax dollars, restaurants and bars generate $880 billion in annual revenue. . . . Without swift action from our local and national leaders, restaurants simply will not be able to weather this storm. But putting direct relief into the hands of business owners is efficient and will have a trickledown effect: from us to our staff and their families; to our farmers, ranchers, and fishermen; to our distributors and suppliers and truck drivers; and then to our communities.[25]

The aspirational message framework used by the Independent Restaurant Coalition:
Aspirational: Save restaurants
Functional: Contribute millions of jobs
Emotional: On the brink of closing
Social: Restaurants anchor every community

The messages developed by the IRC were adopted by media, policy makers, and other advocates for supporting restaurants. In addition to following the aspirational messaging framework, this statement has other key qualities: it is succinct and repeatable. Unfortunately, policy makers don't have the kind of time we need to make complex arguments or to tell them our life stories. Most meetings related to policy change will last less than thirty minutes; sometimes, it could just be a brief interaction. If you can leave them with something quick and memorable, they will use it and repeat it.

Looking back at the relentless work of the IRC, it's clear that the singular argument—that restaurants were too important to fail—resonated with members of Congress. The IRC's call to action to "save restaurants" appeared in the *Congressional Record* more than 150 times from April 2020 to February 2021.

Ask Questions and Connect Aspirations, but Remain Honest and Authentic

It can be daunting to know your audience, develop a story, make it personal and factual (but not too factual), and build lasting relationships, but you can do it. Tackle it like you would a new restaurant opening or the development of next season's menu. Ask yourself a few questions, use the templates included here, and then practice (a lot). Here are the basic questions you need to ask yourself:

- Whom am I trying to reach, and what power do they have make change? Be specific.
- Why am I speaking up, or why do I care? Write down a few sentences that capture why you engage in the cause or what it means to you personally.
- Why does this issue matter to the rest of the world? You need to make audience understand, in just a few words, what is at stake.
- What do I need them to do? Make it clear to your primary audience—the decision makers—exactly what you're asking of them.
- What is the one fact I want to them to remember?
- How will their action make a difference? What will it mean to the world?

Answering these questions will help clarify your argument and prepare you to make a compelling case to policy makers.

On a cautionary note, don't mistake creating a successful argument with fighting with people or debating the facts. My training approach is grounded in the idea of creating conversations, not debates. Debates often devolve into two people talking at each other—think of the presidential debates. Winners are declared based on who lands the most zingers and best articulates their message (and not who answers the question). But rarely do debates change minds. In fact, according to several studies, most people watch debates to "see how their candidate is going to dominate, smear or embarrass the other candidate."[26] Debating—scoring points—makes us feel good, but it doesn't necessarily help advance our causes.

For every successful effort, there are dozens of examples of what happens when advocates get it wrong. One group of chefs I worked with were thrown out of a congressional office after they got into a heated argument with a member of Congress over more funding for school meal programs. The chefs pushed and pushed, the member felt attacked, and when the conversation reached an impasse, the chefs were asked to leave. It is almost impossible to convince anyone to do anything, but you can help them see themselves as part of the solution (or even that it was all their idea).

Ultimately, it is our job to create the conditions for change and bring as many people along and to our side as possible. Honing our audience, sharing our stories, and attaching to our collective aspirations will help us do just that.

Spotlight: Chefs Join the Fight for Healthy Kids

The distinction between presenting a political argument and aspirational messaging can be seen in former First Lady Michelle Obama's approach to advocating for children's nutrition. With more than thirty-one million children participating in the National School Lunch Program and more than eleven million participating in the National School Breakfast Program in 2009, Obama and her team sought to improve the meals that kids were getting at school. Working with members of Congress and industry groups, Obama pushed for a new law that mandated more fruits and vegetables, more whole grains, and less sodium in school lunches in exchange for more federal funding for those meals.

The policy was incredibly controversial, and the White House needed help making the case for the policy change with members of Congress. Obama recruited celebrity spokespeople such as Oprah Winfrey and celebrity chefs to assist with outreach efforts.

Then, on June 4, 2010, she welcomed hundreds of chefs from around the United States to the South Lawn of the White House. The chefs present, part of a larger community of several thousand recruited by the Obama administration, were dressed not in business suits or dresses but chef coats and even toques. All were championed by Obama as experts and influencers. "Each of you has so much to offer when it comes to helping our children make healthy choices. You know more about food than almost anyone—other than the grandmas—and you've got the visibility and the enthusiasm to match that knowledge. That's really what's key," said Obama.[27]

That day put chefs on the biggest political stage in the world and showcased how their voices could be used to accelerate changes in food policy. Armed with aspirational talking points and supported by a well-funded public relations campaign, chefs called for school districts to return to scratch-cooked meals and move away from processed foods. They also advocated for less salt, sugar, dairy, and white flour in school meals. Chefs appeared on talk shows, wrote op-eds for local papers, and signed up to teach cooking classes and counsel parents and students.

A few months later, in December 2010, President Barack Obama signed the Healthy, Hunger-Free Kids Act. The act contained national nutritional guidelines for school meals across the United States.[28]

The Obamas weren't the first to recognize the power of chefs to change the conversation about what kids and families should eat. It also wasn't the first time a chef had engaged in activism. Chef Leah Chase hosted leaders of the civil rights movement throughout the 1950s and 1960s at her New Orleans restaurant Dooky Chase. Chefs Alice Waters and Nora Pouillon educated their guests—including presidents, governors, and members of Congress—about organic and local sourcing. And before chef Kass became Obama's top food advisor, a Black woman, Elizabeth "Lizzie" McDuffie, was both a part-time cook and liaison to the African American community for President Franklin Roosevelt.

None of the actions of any of these chefs was overtly political or partisan, but they had profound implications for policy. The chefs standing on the White House lawn that early June day knew their audience, honed their messages, and as a result, made our food system a little healthier, greener, and more just.

Chapter 4

Make the Ask, Recruit Allies, and Take Action

People coming together to share a meal is a common
denominator that is extraordinarily powerful. I can't
stress enough how you [chefs] are part of the
salvation in terms of bringing people together
on things that matter, that don't have to be
red state, blue state, or partisan.
—*US Representative Earl Blumenauer*[1]

I have worked in Washington, DC, and on policy
advocacy efforts for longer than I care to admit. One thing
that still surprises me is how lobbying meetings work.
When members of Congress are weighing a bill or policy
change, their staff will often accept meetings with interested groups. The key word here is *staff*. It doesn't matter
how large or influential the organization is; rarely is the

first (or even second) meeting with the elected official.

With chefs, it is simply different. Aside from movie stars, chefs are the only group of people that I have seen consistently secure meetings directly with a member of Congress. These meetings often go beyond a quick selfie and focus on what the chef is hearing from others in the community. There is the occasional ask for a reservation or the discussion of a favorite dish, but most of the time the meeting includes a meaningful conversation about the issue.

More than once, a lobbyist has eyed me suspiciously after a powerful elected official has agreed to meet with a chef and has said that that had never happened before. Some believe it's because chefs are considered rock stars and celebrities. When I started working with this community, I thought that, too. Over time, I've learned that while some chefs (and food personalities) are instantly recognizable, the real reason for the special attention is that you are part of a vast network of people and businesses that touch every aspect of the food system (and our individual lives). You are also an important part of your city and neighborhood. You are as visible on Main Street as you are in your restaurant. And, of special consideration for members of Congress, you are likely to be a constituent (and voter) in the district or state they represent.

This network is your superpower when it comes to advocacy. In policy conversations, you often represent not only your own ideas, but also those of the people directly in the communities your elected officials serve. Unlike a paid lobbyist or professional advocate who might live in the Washington, DC, area, far from the issues or organizations they represent, when you talk to a member of Congress, you typically represent a broad network of people who live and work in their electorate.

Tapping into this network of people and finding ways for them to actively engage with you and your advocacy efforts is one of the biggest challenges (but also a huge opportunity) that many chefs face. As one chef said to me, it's easy to decide what's important to me, but it's another thing to ask friends, staff, and connections to come along for the ride. Yet, it is a critical step. Your network is the first place to look for allies: the people and groups that share your interests.

Just like you need people in the kitchen, you need people by your side when talking with elected officials. The more help you have, the more you can achieve. You cannot—and should not—fly solo.

Thankfully, this area is one of the few spots where you don't have to begin from nothing. In addition to your personal networks, including your farmers, staffs, customers, and media relationships, there are scientists, interest groups, charities and other advocates working in every area of the food system.

You can also turn to organizations such as the Independent Restaurant Coalition (IRC), the James Beard Foundation, No Kid Hungry, High Road Restaurants, and dozens of other groups to help you find others working on the issues you care about. You can turn to Google, Instagram, and Twitter to do quick searches. I've included a list of chef-led organizations in the appendix.

In her work around the Supplemental Nutrition Assistance Program (SNAP) and hunger, chef Elle Simone said, "It was at the farmers' market that I was able to meet anti-hunger advocates, agriculturalists, and other SNAP recipients."[2] These people all worked together to prevent the cuts to SNAP in 2016 and will likely continue to collaborate every time the program is attacked. When chefs Steven Satterfield, Mourad Lahlou, and Tiffany Derry started working on food waste, dozens of groups were already working on the issue, and resource directories and websites had been set up so that advocates could easily find one another. When the chefs and owners started IRC, they connected quickly with friends and peers in all fifty states, territories, and every congressional district.

"All the people I have met over the years from culinary school to my time on *Top Chef* to opening my own restaurants—they are all part of my network, and I was used to relying on them for advice or to promote a project that I'm working on. I didn't realize they could also help us when we started the IRC," said chef Kwame Onwuachi. "But then, Tom [Colicchio] called me to join the save restaurants campaign. I couldn't say no to him. The team asked me and all the chefs to help bring other people into the fight. We all just opened up our phones and started asking everyone we knew to help, and it took off." He explained that "it was the same when we started looking for other people to call Congress. The IRC ran an online training, sort of like the Chef Bootcamp. I attended, and after, we all used our contacts to bombard Congress with messages. I don't think they expected it or had seen anything like it before from our community."[3]

Center the Communities You're Trying to Help

If you do the research to learn who is already working on the issues you care about, you'll avoid making the mistake of bypassing the people, causes, and organizations you're interested in supporting. You'll also avoid being pegged with the worst chef stereotype: the narcissist who cares more about the appearance of doing good than doing it.

To get started, ask yourself, who is affected by this problem or cause I'm working on? List as many groups and people as you can who might be affected and therefore might be collaborators. Other questions you want to ask include the following:

- Who is already working on the issue I care about?
- What are they doing exactly (for example, using their social media, writing op-eds)?
- Who are they centering in the work? Is the organization led by people from the communities most impacted?
- Do I like or respond well to what they are doing?
- What do I like about their work?
- Is there some way to reach them and ask them about working together?

It is also important to ask yourself some questions, too. How can you help these people or organizations succeed? What strengths and benefits do you bring to the cause? What do we all gain by working together? These questions will help you better name your own strengths and weaknesses and help you identify who you can and should be supporting.

One thing you don't have to do is start your own non-profit organization or think you're the first to tackle the problem you're trying to solve. If you look around, you will find like-minded people and groups you can work with.

Listening to what the communities and organizations need can also deepen your understanding of the issues. Chef Mary Sue Milliken has worked with Share Our Strength–No Kid Hungry, PEW Charitable Trusts, and Oxfam on issues including hunger in the United States, antibiotic reform, and climate change. When an issue piques her interest, she first does a bit of research to find out who is involved. "We chefs think we're pretty smart, and we all have strong opinions, but I don't have all the answers. When I start working on an issue, I make sure I look at who is leading the effort, who else is involved, and what value I can bring to the conversation," she said.[4]

Map and Build Your Network

The idea of networking may seem crass or tacky, but that's just because we tend to associate it with self-promotion and ladder climbing. In this case, your focus isn't personal aggrandizement but advancement of a cause. The truth is that networking is a basic building block of any successful advocacy effort. There's nothing wrong with—and in fact, there is something quite empowering about—bringing together as many people, organizations, and campaigns as possible to work toward a set of common goals.

Mapping the organizations or individuals you already know and those you aspire to know is an important first step. Identifying the organizations and people in your existing network helps clarify your strongest links and identify which connections you're missing. This step will prepare you to name potential partners, decide the next steps for working together, recognize opportunities to affect the system in which you want to work, and even uncover barriers for creating change in your community.

I find it helpful to think about the table you're trying to set up and who brings what to the effort. They could include your fans, purveyors, other chefs, friends and family, the media, customers, and employees.

Think broadly; you might not have relationships with every person or organization that you want to contact, and that's okay. Think about who you know or who has a relationship with the people you need to fill out your table. Consider the following:

- **Types of work.** What about what you're proposing or supporting is different from other organizations? If you're interested in efforts that reduce food waste, you could connect with national groups such as the Natural Resources Defense Council or ReFED. Alternatively, you might want to focus locally and find organizations that glean on farms or collect meals from restaurants in your community such as Food Recovery Network. Although it is unlikely that no one is working on the issues you care about, by finding out exactly what is happening, you'll be able to find ways for your support and voice to add additional value.
- **Funding.** Who could contribute to your work? What resources are available to you? Are there brand partnerships that you can use? Do you know

which foundations or companies are involved in the decisions for hunger and SNAP issues? Every advocacy effort is going to need financial resources, so it's good to know where support could come from over time.

- **Visibility.** Can others help you reach a bigger audience? Do they have more social media followers or relationships with the media? We'll talk about this subject in chapter 5; for now, realize that raising awareness about your work is important and is a way you can engage your allies in your work.
- **Expertise.** Are others more knowledgeable about the issues than you? Can they help you better understand what's at stake? Do they have a lived experience with the cause you're interested in? Pulling in various experiences and expertise will provide credibility and deepen your own knowledge.
- **Additional networks.** Who do others know that you don't? Can they help you reach even more people to work with? Think of your networks as an active, undulating community. People will drop off, new folks will come in, and it's an easy ask of your networks to introduce you to others.

As you answer these questions, be as specific as possible and list names, even if it's an aspirational connection. The clearer you are about who you're trying to reach and what you want them to do, the easier it will be to move through your networks and build support for your work.

Once you've built yourself a list of potential allies or partners in the work, you'll want to make sure that they are aligned on the focus of your work. Your strategic goals, priority audiences, and personal argument for why this work is important to you and your community are included.

Now, which person should you contact first? As you develop your list of potential allies, you may discover that there are more people on the list than you can even begin to contact. One way to prioritize your list is to rank your contacts by the amount and kinds of ability or assets they can potentially bring to your group or your cause. Make sure to keep in mind what you're trying to do.

If you're trying to raise millions of dollars for a cause, you need allies with either access to financial resources or the ability to reach others who have money. If you're trying to make sure that people pay attention to an issue, you may need people with connections and relationships with media or expertise with social media. Maybe you're trying to organize a rally or big event. If so, you'll need to recruit people with large networks or organizations with members they can mobilize to show up at a specific time or place.

One of my favorite exercises to use is a power grid—a simple chart that will help you map your networks and stay organized. An example follows of a networking grid on how to map the influence and reach of people in your network developed by a group of chefs working on food waste.

In addition to asking what the people in your networks bring to your cause, ask yourself what you to do to support them and their goals. Some organizations and causes need greater visibility to reach a broader audience. Your social media feed could help them accomplish their goal. Perhaps they need someone to share an experience that humanizes a cause. Or maybe they want to reach more chefs or

How to map the influence and reach of people in your network

Type of Power	Rationale	Person or Organization in Your Network
Reach: Do they have lots of followers or fans?	A person or group with a lot of fans or followers on social media might be able to help make your cause more visible.	Chef friend who was featured on national cooking show
Money: Will they donate money to your issue?	Donated money and other resources are always welcome in achieving your group's goals.	Foundation program officer who comes to the restaurant
Expertise: Do they bring specific expertise or lived experience?	People with specific expertise—and lived experiences—can help humanize complex causes and lend credibility to your work.	Food policy director in the city and area farmers
Network: Are they part of an extensive, organized network?	A group that has lots of other groups in its network is going to have financial resources, credibility, and some political power.	Leaders of local composting group; food policy council members
Skills: Do they have special abilities?	An ally may bring technical skills to your group (think fundraising, legal support, or event planning).	Catering company that produces large events

restaurateurs, and you can access your own networks to help. The most successful relationships are reciprocal and engaged, not just transactional or one-sided. Different people and organizations each offer their own skills and benefits, so it is essential to clarify what you need from them and what you can offer. It's also vital to draw a line between working with people who are committed to working with you and those who are only there because you've offered something in return for your support. This last point takes some practice, but as you delve deeper into advocacy, you will quickly figure out who your natural allies and supporters are.

You may also be surprised by the people you find yourself working with—think back to chef Joy Crump in chapter 3. Her main point of contact was a Republican congressman, but they shared common interests in helping improve the lives of those who live in their community. Your allies may also change over time. When we're working on advocacy efforts, advancing the issue takes time, so know that you may do this networking exercise (and others in this book) several times.

Spotlight: Accelerating Antibiotic Reform

A proponent of natural foods and local producers, chef Mary Sue Milliken has worked for decades to raise awareness about the levels of pesticides, additives, and antibiotics in our food supply. First inspired by watching actor Meryl Streep testify before Congress about a chemical used to prolong the life of apples, Milliken became even more engaged in the early 2000s when scientists found a definitive link between the practice of using antibiotics in industrial food animal production and a growing crisis of antibiotic resistance in humans.[5]

According to research done by the US Food and Drug Administration (FDA), the US Department of Agriculture (USDA), and the US Centers for Disease Control and Prevention, antibiotic resistance is responsible for twenty-five thousand deaths in the European Union and twenty-three thousand deaths in the United States each year. As many as two million individuals in the US develop a drug-resistant infection each year. Experts warn that by 2050, antibiotic resistance may cause ten million deaths every year, surpassing cancer as the leading cause of mortality worldwide.[6]

In response, PEW Charitable Trusts created a consumer-focused campaign, Supermoms Against Superbugs, which features mothers from a variety of professions, including chefs and farmers. One of the first spokespeople recruited was Milliken, who appeared on panels and was featured in videos about the campaign. A relentless campaigner for change, she introduced the issue of antibiotic reform to Chefs Collaborative, the James Beard Foundation, and Slow Food USA.

"In supermarkets and in restaurants, consumer demand for meat and poultry raised without antibiotics is growing. People want to know the food they're eating and feeding to their families was produced without putting the public's health at risk," said Milliken.[7]

She reached into her extensive contact list—a result of more than twenty years in the industry—to help recruit dozens of chefs. The campaign was building momentum, but it needed more people to pay attention to the issue. She turned to the team at PEW, including Dr. Lance Price, a leading researcher and advocate, who explained the science of antibiotic resistance to the people in her network. Milliken also connected PEW to the James Beard Foundation, and antibiotic reform became the subject of the first Chef Bootcamp for Policy and Change.

PEW's ask for the chefs and advocates was to sign a letter to the FDA urging the agency to work with the agriculture and drug industries to better understand how antibiotics are used on farms and to curb their overuse. Milliken's network of chefs and farmers recruited more than three hundred chefs to sign and share the letter. That group helped nearly one thousand people get involved.[8]

"I personally called or emailed every chef, farmer, and food personality I knew and asked them to sign that letter and get involved. It helped that PEW was a credible organization and people like Lance were available to answer questions and provide the information we needed. No one followed us blindly, but no one said no," said Milliken.[9]

Over the course of the two years, chefs took part in lobby days, hosted a series of farm-to-table salon dinners, and recruited hundreds of other chefs to constantly pressure the Obama administration to tackle antibiotic abuse in the industrial food system. And on September 18, 2014, the Obama administration signed an executive order directing key federal departments and agencies to act against the rise in antibiotic-resistant bacteria[10]—a direct result of the network that Milliken helped build, train, and mobilize.

The work on antibiotic reform took more than two years and is ongoing today. The same is true of work to end child hunger, reduce food waste, and deliver aid to the restaurant industry post-COVID. None of these issues is simple, requiring advocates to continue pushing for further reform.

To maintain progress and momentum, you need a healthy network of allies. If you ensure that they are informed and engaged, they will be there when needed. They may also be available to help with other projects and causes. Using your vast network to fuel advocacy efforts is easier if you follow a few simple guidelines:

- *Know exactly what you want the people and organizations to do.* Milliken asked all the people in her network to sign letters of support for the PEW campaign. It was a simple ask and didn't require a lot of her network's time.
- *Don't make assumptions about anyone's interests.* During the work to grow the Superbugs campaign, Milliken and PEW reached out to thousands of people in her network, and not everyone said yes. You have to be prepared that not everyone will agree or be willing to help you.
- *Give them the tools needed for success.* Milliken and PEW made it easy for their allies to get involved by providing email templates, tool kits, and letters to sign. People in the food community are often pressed for time. Help make it easy for them to say yes and help you.
- *Approach new relationships authentically.* Milliken called or emailed each person directly. If it is important enough to ask for help, do it yourself. People in your network trust you, not email bots or generic asks.

- *Build unlikely relationships.* One of the most exciting aspects of networking is how often you uncover—and build—relationships with people you may not have thought of before. On antibiotic reform, the group of chefs expanded to include farmers, ranchers, scientists, homeopaths, and parents. These were all people who cared about the issue but hadn't seen one another as natural allies in the fight.
- *Manage your contacts.* It might be helpful to put your contacts into a spreadsheet and, along with their contact information, include information about the issues important to them or how they might be able to help you. This housekeeping step will make your life easier.

Milliken keeps a running spreadsheet of people she's reached out to over the years to help raise money or advance legislation. This group is the first she turns to when she is working on an issue. "People trust me that when I ask for help it's important and that I've done my own research on the issue. I also let people know what happened after they help," Milliken said.[11]

From Transaction to Advocacy

To empower others to join your effort, you need to give your allies meaningful ways to get involved. That's particularly true for chefs, who are often introduced to advocacy through the transactional world of event fundraising.

A rite of passage for many chefs and restaurateurs is being included in food festivals and fundraisers for organizations such as Share Our Strength. Being invited to participate in these events is proof that they have reached a certain level of name recognition or fame. The invitation validates them, and in exchange, the organization receives some free labor and a delicious meal. There's nothing wrong with this setup, but the key is making sure the event isn't a one-off.

Too often, chefs are exploited by groups who want nothing more from the chef community than to use a chef's celebrity to sell tickets and auction items. These things benefit the charity or foundation but don't necessarily advance your personal advocacy goals. If you're asked to cook at a fundraiser, make sure it is a cause or issue you care about because the organization will perpetually use your name and likeness. Make sure that you know exactly what it is you're getting out of supporting their fundraising efforts, or at least make sure they cover your expenses. For some, the cook-and-schlep fundraising circuit is a dead end, but if done right, fundraising events can lead to a long-term relationship with an organization and more substantive involvement in the cause.

"You can draw a direct line from the first-time cooking at a Share Our Strength—now No Kid Hungry—fundraiser to my other work as an advocate," said chef Tom Colicchio. "I was honored to be asked because at the time, it was a sign that you had arrived as a chef. So, I did that dinner for a few years. Then, they asked me to take part in a media training on how to talk about hunger in America. A few years later, I was on Capitol Hill with them and other chefs talking to members of Congress. I, and other chefs, became part of the team that helped to get things done. That first fundraiser started it all."[12]

Fundraisers, media training, and Capitol Hill visits are classic examples of enlisting chefs in advocacy. but they're not the only ways to engage your network. Getting creative about the actions you ask people to take will give them reasons and inspiration to stay involved. That's true even of tough issues such as immigration or addressing racism and hate.

Standing with Restaurant Workers and Farmworkers

Immigration is an issue of immense importance to the restaurant industry. It is estimated that at least one-fourth of all restaurant workers—and the majority of farmworkers—are immigrants (and many of them are without legal authorization to work). Undocumented immigrants, as a whole, pay billions in taxes and a higher effective tax rate average than the top 1 percent of taxpayers (8 percent versus 5.4 percent).[13] They often work in the back of the house as line cooks, bussers, dishwashers, and janitors; are ineligible for tips and kitchen bonuses; and often work without health care, childcare or other transportation benefits. They are the backbone of the industry, yet they are often made invisible and exploited because of their immigration status.

Since early 2009, the restaurant industry has been subject to increased US Immigration and Customs Enforcement raids, legal action, and investigations. Fear grew when the Trump administration expanded its anti-immigrant strategy. Many restaurants were forced to decide whether to fire reliable, undocumented workers in a tight labor market or keep those employees and risk fines or criminal prosecution.

Chefs Cristina Martinez and Ben Miller, owners of South Philly Barbacoa, saw what was happening and felt they had to do something. The issue was extremely personal to Martinez, who originally lived undocumented when she first arrived from Mexico. She had grown her restaurant into a James Beard Foundation winner for Best Chef: Mid-Atlantic and a must-dine destination for anyone visiting Philadelphia.

Together, Martinez and Miller helped organize the Day Without Immigrant actions in 2017. Originally named the Great American Boycott in the early 2000s, the event was designed to raise awareness of the increased criminalization of immigration in the United States. The chefs reached out to everyone in their community, both in Philadelphia and around the country, asking them to close their restaurants for a day, take part in rallies, and share information about the campaign on social media.[14]

Chef José Andrés took part in the collective action by closing four of his restaurants in Washington, DC, in solidarity with the eleven million undocumented immigrants in the United States. Andrés told news outlets at the time, "It's a way to say we love this country, and we want to show you that we are contributing to this country. . . . We all celebrate the best moments of our lives over food at the table linked to immigrants, and we don't want pity. We want respect."[15]

Thanks to pressure from the community, including Martinez and Miller, the Philadelphia City Council passed a resolution recognizing the contributions of immigrants that read, in part, "Immigrants have had an overwhelming positive impact on Philadelphia. . . . They are responsible for the majority of our Main Street business growth, and they have increased our city's cultural vibrancy in many ways. . . . We encourage everyone to find a way to show that immigrants are welcome in Philadelphia."[16] Furthermore, Martinez and Miller's work inspired other chefs around the country to get involved and to take a deeper look at workers in other parts of the food industry.

Chef Andrea Reusing's staff asked her to close her restaurant, Lantern, for the day, in support of the Day Without Immigrants. That experience and the conversations she had about it with her staff and customers dovetailed with her efforts to support food and restaurant workers in North Carolina and nationally.

"After the 2016 election, people in our community were scared. There were raids, people were unsure what would happen, what they could do legally," Reusing said. "At first, we closed Lantern for the national 'day without immigrants' strike to show solidarity with the people who were being targeted, jailed, and deported. Then, we started making the restaurant available as a place for the community to come together to talk, plan, and work together in support of the families being most impacted by the raids."[17]

A brutal reality of our food system is that most consumers are driven not by conscience but by time and convenience. Although that has led to a greater percentage of food dollars going to restaurants, the shift hasn't benefited workers in any area of the industry. In 1996, consumers spent just 39 percent of their food dollars on food eaten away from home, primarily in restaurants. By 2019, consumer spending in restaurants had risen to 51 percent of food purchases in the United States.[18] Over that same period—nearly a quarter of a century—wages for farm and factory workers remained stagnant. The average annual wage for a food production worker is $33,600 per year, while the average income for farmworkers is even lower, ranging between $15,000 and $17,499.[19]

The working conditions in these sectors are also abysmal. Food processing and farmworkers report higher than average rates of debilitating injuries than other manufacturing jobs, and studies show that the workers often don't report illnesses and injuries out of fear of losing their job or employer retaliation.[20]

In Reusing's North Carolina, more than 150,000 immigrant farm and food-processing workers harvest nearly all the food that is used locally and exported. "I'll be the first to admit that I'm skeptical about how much of a difference one restaurant or even one congressperson can make," Reusing said. "But the daily choices we make about food is one of the few ways we as individuals can make a real impact in the world. As chefs and advocates, we need to think more about how we can be useful to our fellow food workers and work towards a more honest, realistic collaboration."[21]

Responding to Anti-Asian Hate

I first met chef Tim Ma, who has restaurants in the greater Washington, DC, area, while working on food waste and child nutrition. He was a longtime participant in fundraising efforts for Share Our Strength, and he became a zero-waste chef when he learned how much reducing food waste could support his own bottom line. Following the 2021 killing of eight Asian women in Atlanta, Georgia, and a rise in anti-Asian hate speech in the Washington, DC, area, Ma and several other chefs, including Kevin Tien and Danny Lee, started doing more to directly address the racist violence.

"Chefs are hospitable. We get into the industry because we are here to serve and help. When I saw the videos of the AAPI [Asian American Pacific Islander] attacks caused by the increased anti-Asian sentiment, I thought, 'that looks like my mom, my dad, my grandparents, getting bullied," said Ma. "Food is a good way to bridge gaps. Our skill is cooking, so we wanted to cook to raise money. It all started with one dinner with five Asian American chefs in DC and is now a network of over two hundred chefs in DC, New York, San Francisco, and Detroit fundraising for local AAPI nonprofits."[22]

The efforts go beyond fundraising. Tien and Ma created Chefs Stopping AAPI Hate, a nonprofit organization focused on raising awareness of violence toward Asian communities. Lee works directly with Embrace Race to promote diversity and equity trainings and promote education to end racial violence. All three men continue to meet with policy makers in Washington, DC, to ensure that the community's voice is heard on safety and racial equity issues.

Inspiring Your Community to Get Involved

Think about the first club or organization you ever joined or the first time an issue motivated you think about getting involved. How did you come across this group? What made you care about its work? What prompted you to participate? If you're like most people, you got involved because the issue became not just an abstraction, but something tangible with real-world consequences.

Ma first got involved in antihunger issues and food waste because it was personal, and his own experiences with anti-Asian violence spurred his creation of Chefs Stopping AAPI Hate. "I have three kids. Looking at my own kids, we are lucky enough as they have not had to deal with food insecurity. It's hard to see any kid go without food," he said. "I did a lot of work early on around food waste and food insecurity. I was always drawn to that. It's the responsibility of a chef to not just be in charge of your kitchen, you're a community leader. I grew up pretty poor and remember being a child and how scarce things were and how hard that is, how hard of a way that is to live."[23]

Martinez and Miller were personally affected by immigration policy and racism. Reusing was not herself an immigrant or farmworker, but she learned the stories of those who were. And the more Colicchio learned about hunger in the United States, the more it seemed like a problem that he could help solve. He said, "Chefs are kind of first responders, and a lot of chefs rally around hunger issues."[24]

"I thought I kind of understood the issue. Then, about six or seven years ago, my wife was mentoring a young girl who had some learning disabilities. Her school didn't have a lunch or breakfast program, and she wasn't eating," Colicchio explained. "My wife is a filmmaker and writer, and she said she wanted to explore this issue. And very quickly, when she started doing the research, we found that people are hungry in this country not because there's not enough food here. It's not because of drought, and it's not because of famine or war. It's because we don't have the political will to make sure that every single person is fed. We can end hunger in this country. There are a lot of intractable problems and issues that we can't fix, but we can end hunger."[25]

The solutions required are complicated and challenging, and not everyone is eager to get involved. Although many of your friends and colleagues may share your values, it doesn't mean that they will join a campaign or organization. In fact, most people don't.

They will tell you they are too busy. They will say it's not their issue. Your job is to inspire them to help you and make it clear exactly what you want them to do.

Tell them why they are important. It might seem obvious, but people need to understand why you need their help (and how they can have influence). Make sure that you really do the work to map out your networks and identify what you need from the community and that your asks are personal, not generic. A general ask is the email you send to ten thousand people asking them to buy tickets to an event. No one on that list feels special or unique. But if you reach out directly to ten or one hundred people with a personal ask, tailored to their expertise and interests, you'll get better responses.

Start small. These are your friends, fans, or colleagues. They already feel a connection to you and your work. You just need to give them the opportunity to engage. For many, engagement is on social media. If you publish meaningful content, others can show support or share it, and this simple act creates an opening. Ma started posting about his firsthand experiences with hate speech and the rising trend of anti-Asian violence. People on his feed could find information and learn about people who were directly affected. Although social media followers might not immediately act, getting information in front of people is an important first step.

Ask for something specific. Once people trust you as a source of information and understand how you're connected to the issue, they may be ready to go deeper. Tell them directly how your work makes a difference. Then, offer opportunities to get more involved—through participating in a fundraiser, volunteering at a function, or attending an event. Whatever the action is, focus on creating a community with your supporters.

Change doesn't happen overnight. There will be many ways for people to get involved, at different times. Make sure to keep your community informed about how their efforts are contributing to the cause. Report on your accomplishments: tell them how much money you've raised, explain where that money went and what it accomplished, and highlight meetings that happened because of your work. Always reinforce a sense of inclusion and emphasize that your work is part of a broader effort.

Recognize contributions. No matter what people do, it's vital to continuously define and celebrate how their actions made a difference. By acknowledging their good work, you'll inspire their continued support and belief in the community you've brought together.

Moving people from interest in an issue to action for your cause isn't always quick or easy. But when it happens, it creates a lifelong community of supporters committed to creating change.

Say "Thank You"

It is impossible to overstate the power of saying "Thank you." In trainings, when I ask the room how many people have been asked to cook at a charity function, all hands go up. Inevitably, everyone has participated in at least one (and often several) of these events. Yet, when I ask how many received thank-you cards or messages, almost no one raises their hand. That's unacceptable. Chefs and farmers that support causes should both be properly compensated for their time, labor, and ingredients (if for an event) and thanked for their time.

It's no different with your allies and friends. If you've asked them to help you raise money, sign a petition, show up for a rally, or reach out to members of Congress, you need to thank them and acknowledge their time, even if that time didn't work out the way you thought it would. A simple "Thank you" will show your allies that you respect them and their efforts.

Milliken said, "I always try to follow up with an email or text, or maybe even a Tweet. I know I appreciate it when someone thanks me, so I make sure to do it. It goes a long way in making sure they will come along with me on the next cause or campaign."[26]

Spotlight: Chef Duskie Estes

Over the years, I've witnessed dozens of live animal harvests, and those experiences changed how I think about the
meat I serve at home or buy at a restaurant. After watching
the life drain from an animal and learning about the options
available to us as consumers, my family changed where we
buy meat and how much we eat. Our consolidated meat
industry makes those types of decisions expensive—and a
privilege. Like me, most chefs change their buying habits
after spending time on a ranch or a kill floor. But supply-
chain issues, state and federal regulations, and cost often
stymied us.

Few chefs that I know have worked as hard and directly
as chef Duskie Estes, a farmer and restaurateur in Sonoma
County, to change the laws that control our meat supply.
Her work starts with taking personal responsibility for her
education and choices. "Take responsibility for the path of
your dollar: don't buy commodity meat. When I go somewhere and I don't know how the meat was sourced, I eat
vegetarian food. When you go to a grocery store, don't buy
meat if they can't tell you where it came from or how it was
treated," she advised. "We don't need to eat eight to twelve
ounces of meat at a meal—three is fine. So, eat less meat,
eat more vegetables, and only allow yourself the right kind
of product."[27]

She also works with the small to midsize ranchers in
Northern California who formed the Bay Area Ranchers
Co-Operative (BAR-C). The group formed after Marin
Sun Farms, the only US Department of Agriculture
(USDA)–certified facility in the Bay Area, announced in

December 2019 that it would no longer process animals for private rancher–owned labels. Some ranchers quit raising livestock for meat rather than undertake the alternative of trucking their animals up to 250 miles away to slaughterhouses in the Central Valley and Eureka. According to Estes, a dozen Sonoma County ranchers logged 26,150 miles making those trips, the equivalent of driving around the world.[28]

BAR-C works to change the policies and regulations in place that create bottlenecks in the supply chain and to end the requirement that all animal producers use USDA-approved slaughtering facilities in the state. The negative impact of these policies reverberates through farms and communities across the country, impacts the health of animals that must be shipped hundreds of miles away from where they are raised, and contributes to climate change.

Ultimately, BAR-C's success rides on the members' ability to reach those in power—something Estes helps organize. She reaches out to her broad networks—including politicians, ranchers, and farmers—with a concrete set of asks, thanks them for their attention, and reaches out again, and again.

"I organized calls with our congressman Jared Huffman, and one with our state assemblyman Marc Levine. We asked Huffman to reintroduce the Prime Act, which he had previously supported. We asked for broader use of the USDA exemptions for poultry and for exemptions for four-legged animals based on the same model. We asked Mark Levine to enable farmers to take advantage of the on-farm poultry slaughter exemptions statewide rather than fighting battles county by county," she said. "I'm maxed out. In my own business, family, and farming, I try to make time to follow up whenever I have a free moment. I spent months emailing all these people to try to get people to our meetings, and it's awesome because they actually show up. And we're making progress."[29]

In February 2022, Estes and US Department of Agriculture Undersecretary Jenny Lester Moffitt were present when BAR-C announced the opening of the first-of-their-kind mobile meat processing units that would serve more than eighty ranchers in the Bay Area.

"This is the future of regenerative agriculture and farming, and we built it from within our community. We saw a problem and we fought to solve it," said Estes. "Together, we helped to change the lives and livelihoods of folks in our community, and we will get to see the results of that work every day."[30]

Chapter 5

Grab Attention and Break Through

When they work on issues they care about, chefs can break through all the chaos and reach different audiences. When chefs take a stand, people notice. The media notices. They get a different reaction than most, and the causes and campaigns they work on benefit from their voice being in the mix.
—*Kristopher Moon, chief operating officer and president of the James Beard Foundation*[1]

A lot of hard, thoughtful work goes into developing your personal advocacy strategy. It's very much like designing your first menu, writing a cookbook, or building out a restaurant. As described in the previous chapters, your recipe for advocacy requires focusing on the issue you care about deeply, identifying your audience and what you want them to do, and rallying your allies to act. In this chapter, we'll focus on the medium for your advocacy—in other words, the media and other channels you can use to communicate your message to your audience and ask your allies to participate. Like any advocate, your biggest challenge is getting others to pay attention.

When you're marketing your new book—or your new restaurant—you need to design a communications strategy and find ways to get your message into the universe. Your goal is to get as many butts in seats as you can. The same is true with advocacy. Advocacy doesn't mean shouting into the void or trying to grab the attention of that fictitious group known as "the general public." It does, however, mean reaching as many people within your target audience and ally groups as possible. And that requires effectively using the channels available to you.

When it comes to advocacy, the medium isn't necessarily the message. It's easy to look out at the media landscape, from makeup tutorials on Instagram to cat videos on Tik-Tok (cute as they are), and dismiss it all as superficial. I know many of you chafe at the idea of celebrity chefs and foodies. No one who is serious about their craft wants to be more famous for being famous than they are for cooking. Even the word *foodie* is synonymous with *poseur*—at least that's how one chef described it to me when I once used the term to describe myself and my husband. (That will never happen again!)

Celebrity-driven food media is nevertheless all around us and is a dominant part of our culture. There are more than 3.6 billion social media accounts in the world,[2] and the hashtag #food has more than three hundred and eighty million impressions.[3] These accounts influence food trends and shape how we shop. During the second week of February

2021, feta cheese was the top-trending search term on Google. If you're under thirty, you know exactly what was behind this search: a TikTok post in which people baked feta cheese with cherry tomatoes and then combined them with pasta for a quick dinner. This pasta dish got more than six hundred and sixty million views around the world in just a few months, with real ramifications to the supply chain. Supermarkets from Charlotte, North Carolina, to Jersey City, New Jersey, to Sydney, Australia, couldn't keep the salty Greek cheese in stock. Similar shortages occurred with the other main ingredients.[4] That is how fast—and influentially—a topic can take off in the world of food media.

More weighty topics can also move quickly through food media. In April 2021, the *New York Times* published an investigation of Willows Inn on Lummi Island in the Pacific Northwest.[5] The story revealed that the James Beard Award–winning restaurant was home to multiple allegations of racist bullying, wage theft, and sexual harassment allegedly committed by its chef and management. Also, despite its long-stated (and lauded) philosophy to source locally and organically, the restaurant used commercial, conventionally raised poultry and produce. Food media rightly pounced on the story, and leaders in the industry condemned the hypocrisy and dishonesty of the restaurant's leadership.

The Restaurant Manifesto, a website and Twitter feed written by Adam Reiner, posted, "In this Willows Inn story, we shouldn't overlook the GM's [general manager's] complicity (Reid Johnson). Abusive chefs always surround themselves with lieutenants that're willing to look away. Mr. Johnson's job was to bury the skeletons, not run a restaurant. Chefs like Blaine Wetzel don't work alone."[6]

There were follow-up stories in *Bon Appétit* and the *Seattle Times*. Social media influencers, including Reiner and chef Preeti Mistry, publicly supported the more than thirty-five employees who reported the abuse. Multiple lawsuits were filed by staff members, and at least one settled for more than $1 million.[7] The restaurant closed just over a year later, in December 2022.

Remember that what happens in your restaurant or online doesn't stay there. In today's world, you cannot hide, and there are real-world consequences to your choices, behavior, and the channels you use to communicate. Food media can shape trends and can accelerate changes in the industry. It is up to you to find the best way to harness its power, and your own platform, to advance the causes you care about.

A Crowded Landscape

Despite the influence of food media, it is incredibly hard for political and policy advocacy to break through. Keep in mind that you're competing against hundreds of different causes and campaigns, millions of vlogs, videos, and pictures, and billions of advertising dollars for products, brands, and events. Pulling attention toward your cause takes effort.

When I first started working in Democratic politics in the early 1990s, there were only a few different ways to reach voters: television and radio advertisements, stories on one of a dozen or so television networks, direct mail, and in-person events. Since then, the number of ways for people to find information has exploded. First came twenty-four-hour cable news and talk radio. Then it was online chat rooms and news feeds, and now people can instantaneously access news and information from thousands of sources, including social media, podcasts, email newsletters, and text messages.

Today, even traditional news media, such as NBC or the *New York Times*, also invest in multiple platforms, including YouTube, Facebook, and Twitter, to reach audiences. The *Los Angeles Times* has a TikTok channel, and the Food Network has a magazine and multiple digital channels.

All that adds up to an incredibly crowded landscape. The way we're consuming all this information is rapidly changing, too. A 2010 study showed that the average person spent more than fifty-seven minutes a day consuming news and information using traditional media sources such as newspapers.[8] Today, our print and traditional media use has plummeted, but social media is on the rise. People spend an average of two and a half hours every day monitoring and interacting on social media, including Twitter, Instagram, and TikTok.[9]

One statistic that keeps me optimistic about advocacy messages capturing people's attention—even on a tiny screen—is that demand is growing for leaders and companies to have a point of view on social and environmental issues. One brand survey found that when consumers know that a company is environmentally friendly, they are more likely to support it, and 64 percent of Millennial and Gen Z consumers want brands to take socially conscious stands.[10] Although that survey used raw marketing data, it points to an opening for industry leaders—including chefs—to talk about important causes.

Communication Channels

A positive way to look at today's crowded media landscape is that you have a multitude of channels to reach your audiences and allies, but there are key differences between them. It's important to recognize each channel's value (and pitfalls), pick those that are right for you and your cause, and craft your strategy to fit your preferred channel.

When we think of a communications strategy, we tend to think of news/mass media (newspapers, websites, television), or social media (Facebook, Instagram, TikTok, and the like). Although those channels can have significant impact, they aren't the only ones. A communications channel can be as flashy as a billboard or as simple as a one-on-one conversation. We'll delve into the variety below, starting with media and electronic communications. If your preferences lean toward luddite, don't worry—there are also IRL (in real life) options.

- **Social media.** There's a reason social media is at the heart of many successful communications strategies: it is immediate, curated, authentic (or at least it can feel that way), and very easy to share. It is tailor-made for you to communicate information, fundraise, and ask people to support your work. Later in this chapter, we'll look at examples of harnessing social media for good, but we already know a few reasons it is such a powerful tool. It is, as we've discussed, the number one platform for food-related content. It offers a convenient way to share pictures, stories, how-to videos, and behind-the-scenes looks at your advocacy efforts. You can connect with your audience on the platforms where you both spend the most time. Thanks to the way social media channels are set up, they are also incredibly efficient (and often free or low-cost) ways to reach a large audience and allow that audience to interact with you. Using social media has some disadvantages, too, including the need to deal with trolls, keep posting relevant content, and even keep up with constantly changing platforms, but the power to reach millions with your messages and directly engage with people often outweighs those challenges.

- **Emails.** Chefs tend to have a large number of personal contacts that you can reach out to personally. Chef Mary Sue Milliken took her email list of thousands of chefs and engaged them in her work to curb antibiotic use (see chapter 4). To reach chefs with updates and messages about food waste, organizing chefs emailed tens of thousands of chefs, restaurateurs, Chef Action Network members, and alumni of the Chef Bootcamp for Policy and Change. This individualized touch is amazingly effective, and it is one of the few communications channels with which you can easily track whether people are opening your messages and responding. Use it sparingly, and make sure you respect your recipients' privacy. Just because someone signed up for a marketing email from your restaurant or gave you their contact info at a festival doesn't mean that they want your unsolicited policy updates, nor does it mean they've given you permission to share their information with others. If someone asks to come off your lists, take them off immediately and never share their email address (or any other information) without their explicit permission. Also, the average person gets more than 150 emails a day, and a good percentage of those have an "ask"—buy this, read that, take this action—meaning that email is another crowded channel. Think of email like nutmeg: a little goes a long way.

- **Text messages.** One of the things I've learned over the years is to follow up any email ask with a quick text message. Aside from a phone call, texting is the most personal and immediate form of communication and one that every chef relies on to prioritize your day. It's also increasingly a medium that advocacy groups are using to send quick asks for money and actions. Like email, you can tell when a message is delivered and opened. Some studies show that the open rate is 90 percent with text messages (compared to the 55 percent of email that goes unread).[11] It is a medium that relies on brevity and immediacy. Messages such as "Sign the petition I just emailed you" or "Call your member of Congress tomorrow" work, to a point. Even more than email addresses, you want to treat phone numbers with care. Never send group text messages about advocacy, don't bombard people with messages, and never share a person's information with anyone unless that person has agreed to it in advance. If emails are like nutmeg, think of text messages like white truffles.

- **News/mass media.** Some may think that only true celebrity chefs get asked to be on television, but the demand for food content means that on almost any given day in the United States, you'll find a chef or restaurateur on television. Chefs are more prepared than most to use your public relations platforms and media opportunities to raise awareness of issues. All the requests to demonstrate a recipe or talk about new restaurants can be turned into an opportunity to bring attention to your cause. When chef Michael Cimarusti appears on any show, he highlights his approach to locally sourced seafood and the work of partnerships such as Dock to Dish. When considering which fishes to highlight in a recipe or cookbook, chef Renee Erickson takes the opportunity to focus on sustainable seafood options. This approach keeps chefs in the public eye and ensures that topics like seafood sustainability reach a broad audience. Publishing op-eds, such as chef Elle Simone's on childhood hunger, are another opportunity to use media platforms to share your story.
- **Paid media campaigns.** This strategy is usually not something that any one chef can sponsor or set up. The cost of public service announcements (PSAs) or other forms of paid advertising are often out of reach, but there are ways to make them happen. By partnering with larger nonprofit organizations, you

might get an opportunity to share your story as part of their advocacy efforts. Another approach is working with food brands equally committed to social or policy change. The Independent Restaurant Coalition (IRC) partnered with several brands and companies committed to "saving restaurants" during the pandemic, including airing a series of advertisements and PSAs that ran on national television and radio stations throughout 2020. Ads sponsored by San Pellegrino and liquor-brand Cointreau, urging people to patronize local restaurants and to support the RESTAURANTS Act, aired as part of *Top Chef* and even the Super Bowl.

- **One-on-one communication.** In the real-life category, there's really no better way to reach an individual than through a personal conversation. One place that might happen is in your restaurant. Politicians and their staffs eat out, just like the rest of us. To get the conversation started, there is nothing wrong with asking them if they would like a tour of the kitchen or even visiting them at their table. Like many customers, they may wave you off or ask to just have dinner, but you can use that opportunity to request a one-on-one meeting. As a constituent, you can also just reach out to an office and ask to meet with the staff or elected official. People are always surprised, but of all the people I've worked with on policy advocacy, chefs tend to be able to snag meetings that not even paid lobbyists can get. Think of chef Michel Nischan's work on hunger issues or even the meetings that chefs

Steven Satterfield, Mourad Lahlou, and Tiffany Derry held on food waste. This work required direct contact with policy makers. These types of meetings typically won't last long and require that you have a strong message and simple ask. Make sure you know what you want to get out of the meeting and ask for it. Don't expect the official to come prepared to decide on your issue, so be sure to have plans to follow up. This type of outreach is time-consuming, but it is the most effective form of advocacy when dealing with elected officials and policy makers. They want to hear from their constituents and supporters, first and in person.

- **Community events.** Allied organizations—the groups you've identified and started to work with—have audiences all their own. Over time, you may have the opportunity to meet with a group's members or supporters. It's likely that these people will already be on your side and that you share common approaches or opinions. One simple option is to say yes when asked to cook at fundraisers, rallies, or even conferences that align with your views. Or you can take control, reach out to organizations you're interested in working with, and offer to help organize events. When pushing for more gardens in schools, chef Charleen Badman in Arizona hosted regular gatherings for chefs and others. These gatherings grew into a series of educational sessions that helped strengthen relationships between parents, teachers, and chefs and led to an annual fundraiser and community event. Being proactive allowed

Badman to take more control of the discussion. Instead of being "just a cook" at an event, she is a leader and is responsible for the messages, activities, and strategy she uses.

- **Nontraditional communications.** Sometimes, the normal channels or opportunities are insufficient or take much more time or money than you have to give. There are many other ways that you can reach people, however. Within your restaurant, you can put messages on the menu or on tent cards on your tables. Even signs in the window work. Also, consider all the opportunities that present themselves during service to highlight issues important to you. During the IRC's fight for the restaurant relief bill, a flyer was created for restaurants to staple to every order urging customers to call their member of Congress. One of my favorite things for chefs and restaurateurs to do is ask someone to tour the kitchen. One of chef Joy Crump's first conversations with her US representative, Tom Wittman, was at her restaurant in Fredericksburg, Virginia. There, she felt most comfortable approaching a member of Congress and talking to him about a contentious issue.

Choosing which of these tools to use is going to take some work. A simple rule of thumb is to figure out where you and your audiences interact most and go from there.

Be Yourself

No matter what communications channels you employ, you need to show up in ways that are true to you and your personality—a trait that comes naturally to many chefs and culinary professionals. For example, chef Badman's annual event in Scottsdale, Arizona, doesn't include any chef coats or stuffy kitchens. The hundreds of participants, including business leaders, state legislators, school super-intendents, teachers, and parents, are casual, and the event feels like a backyard picnic. In 2016, when we brought chefs to Washington, DC, we encouraged everyone to wear business casual clothes and leave their toques at home. The vibe was professional and serious but also true to a group of advocates who rarely ever had to wear a suit and tie (or dress and heels).

The appetite for something real and natural—let's call it authentic—is strong and growing. That's especially true in online communications, where everything can feel manufactured.

At the James Beard Foundation, videos, blogs, and social media posts featuring chefs talking about differ-ent campaigns are some of the top shared content by the foundation's more than one million Instagram and Twitter followers. "We see an immediate uptick in engagement when we post about a topic like sustainable seafood or reducing food waste," said Kristopher Moon, president and chief operating officer of the James Beard Foundation. "It's even higher if it's not something we've heavily produced. Our audiences, and the chefs' audiences, want it to feel real and like they are seeing something no one else gets to see. We know a quick selfie or picture with a chef talking to a congressman will get more likes or comments than a canned post on an issue. Being real helps the audiences understand and relate to the issue."[12]

Providing people that behind-the-scenes look at advocacy efforts also helps make the issues more accessible. When chefs Annie Pettry and Hugh Acheson traveled to Washington, DC, to meet with members of Congress in 2019 about childhood hunger, they chronicled their visit on social media. The pictures showed them in front of the Capitol, walking through the halls, and even in selfies with members of Congress. All the posts were tagged with #NoKidHungry and the social media handles for everyone they met with, thus reaching hundreds of thousands of accounts in just a few short hours.

With just a few posts, they were able to bring the IRL activities to a broader audience. This IRL–social media combo also helps you get real-time feedback on your work.

Chef Jenny Dorsey and the team at Studio ATAO, the food policy think tank, use a TikTok channel to host information about their curriculum to end bias in food media and to collect information about what their audience wants to see them take on next. The format also allows them to get almost instantaneous feedback and reach audiences interested in the topic of #foodadvocacy.

"With TikTok and Insta[gram], we can just pop on, post a video, or host a live [stream], and our followers will tell us immediately what resonates. We can engage very differently. We can also see very quickly if something gets shared," said Dorsey. "Social media also allows us a chance to bypass many of the established gatekeepers in food media and advocacy."[13]

Articles Will Help You Find Your People

For communications to really stick, you want people to feel connected to you and the work. Throughout history, we've turned to visual images, including posters, to help us publicly communicate our support of a cause or movement. Elizabeth Resnick, a professor at the Massachusetts College of Art and Design, called this form of communication "dissent made visible" and said that technology has expanded the role of this type of advocacy. "Posters are dissent made visible," she explained. "Technology has exponentially expanded the poster's role well beyond the limitations of the printed surface and has become a core component of 21st Century advocacy."[14] Within the "A Is for Advocacy" framework, we called it the "article"—the visual clue that will help your people find you in the crowded media landscape.

For a whole generation of advocates, ribbons were the most popular form of this iconography, and the color denoted which cause or campaign—red for AIDS funding and research, pink for breast cancer, teal for ovarian cancer. Ribbons gave way to bracelets, and now, in the social media age, objects have been joined by hashtags and pictures on Instagram and Facebook. These virtual signifiers are often still accompanied by old-school hats, T-shirts, and posters. This collection of wearable and shareable items also lets us quickly find other people and groups in the crowd at a protest or virtually online.

Hashtags are the twenty-first-century version of visible advocacy. They not only allow us to show our support for campaigns and causes on social media and make it easy to track who else is sharing the same information, but they also create a way to hold people accountable. In 2006, sexual assault survivor Tarana Burke created the hashtag #MeToo and began to use it on Twitter. In 2017, women (and men) used it all over the world to raise awareness of sexual violence. Included among them were people working in the culinary industry who wanted to change restaurant culture and hold abusers accountable. The hashtag moved quickly and was used more than nineteen million times on Twitter.[15]

Speed is important. Studies show that we often spend fewer than fifteen seconds on a page, but we can also identify and understand an image in as little as thirteen milliseconds. It takes much longer to read and understand a paragraph of text communicating the same thing, time we often don't have when we're trying to explain complicated concepts or get people to join in our work.

Bakers Against Racism is one group that used a hashtag to profound effect to raise money to fight racism through a global bake sale. Organized by chefs Paola Velez, Willa Pelini, and Rob Rubba, the initiative started as a single fundraiser for Minnesota Freedom Fund (a bail fund)[16] and grew to include thousands of bakers who raised more than $2.5 million in small donations in support of Black-led organizations in the summer of 2020.[17]

"I was sad, mad, and frightened by what was happening in the world. I was also unemployed, having been laid off from my job. It all started with a fundraiser we did called

Doña Dona," said Velez. "But I knew we could do more. And I knew there were other bakers, people like me, who just wanted to help."[18]

"It happened quickly. We secured a hashtag and an Instagram and Twitter, and I made a Google doc. It cost zero dollars to make this. Literally, it cost us zero dollars to start this initiative, and I launched it with an image that Robb designed," said Velez. "I knew because I have studied the algorithms that the image needed to get people, catch people's attention. The algorithm would push it out if they stopped scrolling, even for a few seconds. That's how so many people saw it. From there, it just took off."[19]

The chefs were also intentional about their choice of language, and while anyone was free to take part, the message and expectations were clear. "If you shared it or baked, it was clear this was about supporting Black Lives Matter and Black-led organizations. You were showing the world you were against racism. We made it impossible for you to change that, and for anyone buying a baked good from you knew it, too," said Velez.[20]

"With Bakers Against Racism, I really wanted people to get into [it and] instead of it being a hashtag, where you say Black Lives Matter and then you move on, you're baking, you're doing something that's so personal," she continued. "My grandmother taught me how personal it is to cook for somebody. To cook for somebody and feed them is wanting them to live. So, in Bakers Against Racism, I was making a call to action for people to want Black lives to live. And that's why we say Black Lives Matter."[21]

As the campaign spread, bakers were active on five continents, in seventeen countries, forty-one states, and two hundred plus cities.[22] The participants were part of a centuries-old tradition of using bake sales to raise money for social causes and school funds. The story of Georgia Gilmore, a Black cook who used her professional skill and personal networks to raise money during the Montgomery, Alabama, bus boycott, is well known in culinary circles. Women across Montgomery sold plates of pork chops and rice, pound cake, and most famously, sweet potato pies, and proceeds from the sales by "Gilmore's Club from Nowhere" went to pay for transportation for Black workers during the nearly thirteen months of the boycott.[23]

The success of these efforts is tied to their coordinated but decentralized models allowing all participants—professional and amateur bakers—to play to their strengths. That was true of Gilmore's effort, where sales were made with cash only and usually in relative secret. It was also the case of Bakers Against Racism and related bake sales.

"If you have a special skill or special talent, that can also be used as a force of change," Pelini said. "Everybody has a role to play, and you can use what you're good at to push forward the cause."[24]

Give Up Control

Bakers Against Racism is a wildly successful advocacy effort: it raised awareness, resulted in millions of dollars in contributions, and pushed people to join the fight for social justice. At the height of the 2020 presidential election, the community participated in dozens of events for the Biden-Harris campaign and campaigns around the United States. This flexibility was possible because Bakers

Against Racism was a campaign of loosely affiliated efforts and not the brainchild of a DC-based nonprofit organization or advertising company. It was created by, and for, people who identified as antiracist (and bakers).

Bakers Against Racism also followed a model of some of the most effective advocacy efforts:

- Create a simple, repeatable message (Bakers Against Racism).
- Reach out to closest allies and networks (bakers and culinary professionals).
- Give people a straightforward way to get involved (host a bake sale).
- Make it completely transparent (use Instagram and Google).
- Highlight others in the network (share videos).
- Thank followers for their help and ask for more.

Finally, give up trying to control it. Velez, Rubba, and Pelini created a basic structure and tool kit that gave participating bakers all the information they needed to set up their own local events. There were no standards about what participants had to bake and no requirements on the amount of donation or time—or even the organizations that a baker had to support. The audience and mission were clear—Bakers Against Racism—but it was up to each and every person to figure out the best way to be involved.

Ceding control isn't usually something that chefs excel at; it runs counter to what you do in the kitchen every day. But think of it as adapting recipes and ingredients to fit your own style. Open-source advocacy is, in my experience, among the best ways to advance important causes.

In the early 2000s, I led the design of the Nothing But Nets campaign at the United Nations Foundation. In a 2006 *Sports Illustrated* column, Rick Reilly, an award-winning sportswriter, wrote about how placing insecticide-treated nets over beds could protect vulnerable families around the world from malaria and asked readers to contact the foundation for information.[25] Even he was surprised that his readers started sending checks, some as small as $10, to help pay for the bed nets. At the time, relatively few Americans knew that malaria claimed almost a million lives each year and that the solutions to prevent this disease, including bed nets, were cheap to produce and highly effective.

From Reilly's initial column to a campaign that was as simple as the call to action, "send a net," Nothing But Nets raised more than $130 million and provided thirty-nine million of the world's most vulnerable people with bed nets.[26] Nothing But Nets also recruited more than 350,000 individual supporters who organized everything from church fundraisers to sports tournaments. This community effectively advocated for policy change, including increases for lifesaving malaria programs such as the President's Malaria Initiative; the Global Fund to Fight AIDS, Tuberculosis and Malaria (Global Fund); and the United Nations. Nothing But Nets (now called United to Beat Malaria) is just one of the hundreds of campaigns that tap into the creativity and energy of communities to produce powerful results.

Mix It Up and Make It Count

Open-source advocacy isn't for everyone. One constant criticism of online efforts—especially when the primary platform is social media—is that it is a lazy way to participate. Critics will say that true advocacy can only be done by voting or showing up for protests and collective actions.

I absolutely agree, up to a point. Indeed, at times virtual advocacy efforts are shallow, superficial, and don't help advance causes or issues. The world of clicktivism, defined as "involving little or no commitment," is littered with failed campaigns and social-media-only moments. For advocacy to work, you have to use the advantages of social media (for example, immediacy, broad audiences) and mix it up with media efforts and in-real-life interactions. Recipes don't work if you leave out crucial ingredients, whether it's for your favorite dish or policy advocacy.

One instance when chefs helped put together a distinctive mix of meetings, events, social media, and networking involved the contentious world of genetically modified organisms (foods), or GMOs. In the early 2000s, I worked on a project for a global foundation interested in learning more about consumer attitudes about GMOs. After sorting through the reams of public opinion data and transcripts from hundreds of interviews and focus groups, the research team realized that very little could be done to shift perceptions and feelings about GMOs. If you believed that GMOs pose great risks to human health and the environment, industry-funded research reveals nothing that will change your mind. The same is true if you believe that GMOs are perfectly safe and provide a pathway to climate-resilient crops. Again, nothing will sway you. In fact, the immovable opinions about GMOs, the funding on all sides of the debate, and the supporters at every level of government and policy making make it the toughest issue I have ever worked on with the chef community.

From 2012 to 2016, the GMO debate ping-ponged in Congress with bipartisan groups of lawmakers lining up behind two bills, one to require that the US Food and Drug Administration label food products made with GMOs and one to halt any mandatory labeling. For chefs, labeling has implications for marketing and menus, especially those highlighting organic and local foods.

Two chef advocacy groups, Food Policy Action, led by chef Tom Colicchio, and the Chef Action Network, founded by chef Michel Nischan and where I was the founding executive director, helped recruit chefs from around the United States to push for mandatory labeling. The chefs' opinions mirrored public opinion at the time: more than 89 percent of Americans favored GMO labeling.[27]

For more than two years, the chefs engaged in a pitched battle to defeat bills that would have rolled back state laws and made any food labels voluntary—a move that would have affected everything from GMO fruits and vegetables to salmon. The first round of activities included email blasts that went out to chefs asking them to sign a petition reading: "As chefs, we have a fundamental right to know what's in the food we cook and serve to our customers. We urge you to reject any attempt to prevent the mandatory labeling of genetically modified food."[28] From a core group of about twenty chefs, ultimately more than four thousand chefs from around the country signed a petition calling for greater transparency around the use of GMOs.

More than seven hundred of the chefs also traveled to Washington, DC, to meet with members of Congress and staffs at the US Department of Agriculture (USDA) and policy experts in the Obama administration. The chefs came from both fine-dining and casual restaurants across forty-nine states, Washington, DC, Puerto Rico, and the US Virgin Islands. They posted short videos and pictures of their meetings, including selfies with members of Congress, to social media. They also endorsed and signed op-eds, appeared on national television news shows, and appeared at several events around the country, including in cities where the presidential debates were happening that year.

The chefs were important voices. According to several senators, including Senator Tim Kaine (D-VA), "As a Richmond resident, I have frequented many of the restaurants and farms whose proprietors came in to meet this week, and it was valuable to listen to their views. Those visiting my office made a strong case for why Congress should not make it harder for consumers to be informed about what is in the food that they eat."[29]

We didn't have any budget for television or radio ads, so the chefs found other ways to break through using the most available channels—mostly email and social media. It worked. Despite the deep pockets of the pro-GMO lobby, the chefs and advocates were successful in pushing for transparency, including new laws "empowering the USDA to enact a labeling system for what the law calls bioengineered food, defined as food that has been genetically engineered in a way that could not be obtained through conventional breeding or found in nature."[30]

Face the Critics, Head On

Advocacy efforts that result in lasting change demand that we find opportunities to do it all. (I know that is an exhausting concept. Remember that you don't have to do it all at the same time. Do what comes naturally first, then keep going.) Advocacy takes time.

Another thing to remember is that when you break through the clutter and attract attention and new followers, not all of that attention will be positive. For instance, I will always remember the call I received from a famous chef based in Georgia during the lead-up to the presidential election in 2016. The chef was negotiating a major deal with a national brand, and the company was worried about what the chef was posting on social media feeds, particularly Twitter.

Company executives had two concerns about the chef's posts. First, they were concerned that the chef appeared to be losing followers, and second, they were worried that the chef might attract the attention of presidential candidate Donald Trump. The company didn't want to become collateral damage. To their credit, the chef didn't flinch at the idea of engaging with Trump, but we did have a conversation about followers and the impact of the chef's advocacy on their ability to attract national brands.

Not everyone is going to love you, choose to support you, or join you. It is entirely possible, even a given, that you will lose followers. You may find your Yelp reviews or Instagram feeds filled with vitriol and hate. You may get tough questions from customers, fans, or partners.

How you respond is up to you, but if, as I told the chef, you stick to your guns, you may lose some fans but attract others whose beliefs align with your own. In the case of the Atlanta-based chef, over time they attracted new followers who cared about politics and food policy. The original brand decided not to partner with them, but the chef was able to attract the attention of companies interested in supporting their work on social issues. Today, they have a variety of sponsors and work with both national and international brands.

The chefs with whom I worked on GMO reform were attacked online, too. Even though 89 percent of Americans supported labeling efforts, opponents of the work, including several members of Congress, decried the chefs' efforts, refused to take meetings, and even accused them of wanting to drive up the cost of food.

The chefs, whether dealing with potential sponsors or members of Congress, did not back down. Change wouldn't be possible without all the chefs, farmers, owners, and others in the restaurant industry who've chosen to use their voice to challenge decades, if not centuries, of entrenched thinking, behavior, practices, and policy.

When I need further inspiration on this point, I look to people such as chef Mistry. They are a James Beard Foundation Best Chefs in America semifinalist for their Oakland restaurant and cookbook author, and they self-identify as an "activist" on social media and in public forums. "As a queer brown immigrant chef, I have no interest in backing down. Revolutions were not staged without making someone uncomfortable. Rights were not gained by accepting the status quo," said Mistry.[31]

Track Your Progress

The time it takes for your efforts to be successful will absolutely vary depending on what issues you focus on, who you engage with, and how much time you dedicate to advocacy. Changing the way your restaurant operates usually takes the least amount of time because it's largely in your hands. You can make the decision to switch suppliers or communicate differently with your staff. In the case of policy change, you're not in control. It could be years before a bill becomes a law or a regulation is updated.

Measuring advocacy success is quite different from the way you would measure success in your restaurant. If you're gauging your restaurant's profitability, you can chart sales and expenses almost up to the minute. That's not the case with advocacy, but it doesn't mean that you shouldn't try to track your own work and the progress of the issue you've chosen.

Although not particularly easy or straightforward, there are ways to gauge the effectiveness of your advocacy. They include tracking audience engagement with your social media posts, recording any meetings with policy makers and their staffs, setting up media searches such as Google News alerts to capture any media mentions, and tracking the open rate on any email communications you send.

Tracking your progress will help you understand if your messaging needs to be tweaked or if one type of communications channel has more impact than another. Maybe you'll learn that your Instagram account gets tons of engagement, but that few people are opening your newsletter—or vice versa. This knowledge will help you make informed decisions about where to concentrate your efforts and will ultimately allow you to build deeper engagement with your audiences, allies, and partners.

Chef Velez of Bakers Against Racism described how tracking progress can create a virtuous cycle. "When Bakers launched, we could see every time a post was tagged and shared. At one point, we could tell that more people were sharing one image on Instagram, so we made that image in a variety of assorted colors. We also changed up some of our messaging to make it clearer about what we wanted the bakers to do," she explained. "Because we were primarily on social, we could update everyone on how much money was raised almost instantly. That then got people even more excited. By tracking everything, and sharing it back out, the bakers got really excited, and more and more people got involved."[32]

Spotlight: Anthony Myint and Zero Food Print

When I consider how chefs can navigate the ever-changing communications landscape and balance the many activities that add up to successful advocacy, I think about chef Anthony Myint. I first experienced Myint's food when he was the chef at Mission Street Food in San Francisco and Mission Chinese in New York City. Myint and another chef, Danny Bowien, originally built the restaurants to raise money for causes, including antihunger efforts. We invited Myint to a Chef Bootcamp for Policy and Change a few years later, and by that time he had begun to think about food, climate change, and the ways restaurants could help reduce greenhouse gas emissions.

Myint, Karen Leibowitz, Myint's wife and partner, and two friends started a nonprofit organization, Zero Foodprint (ZFP). The organization's original mission was to help restaurants reduce their own climate footprint. Dozens of restaurants worked with the organization to audit their operations, but the project really took off when, during the Global Climate Action Summit in 2018, ZFO recruited more than forty Bay Area restaurants to go climate neutral for a week. That effort led to deeper engagement with restaurants and San Francisco diners.

It also helped Myint and his partners realize how long it would take to sign up hundreds and thousands of restaurants, so they began to look for other ways to engage chefs and restaurateurs in climate solutions. "Basically, no chefs were working on climate change when we started," said Myint. "We were able to get that first group involved, but it takes a lot of time to onboard chefs, get them thinking about ways to change, and the system isn't really set up to help them or farmers transition. It's also incredibly complex. Not everyone wanted to get deep into soil science with us. So, we found another way, and that's led to changes in how money flows from customers to restaurants to farms, and to policy change."[33]

To empower more chefs and customers to engage with complex climate solutions, Myint and the ZFP team created the Restore California campaign. Restaurants add a 1-percent surcharge to customer bills. The money is collected by ZFP and distributed to farmers growing food with a focus on replenishing the soil's health. This program offers diners a way to directly fund carbon farming projects such as compost application, cover crop planting, tree planting, and improved grazing management.

"From a standpoint of food activism, Zero Foodprint is a really easy way for me to be active, and it starts with the dialogue I have with my team in the restaurant," said chef Daniel Asher, a chef in Colorado and a participant in the ZFP program. "They are our frontline ambassadors as they get the questions from customers about the surcharge. I hear them having conversations, and the impact that I've seen in the period of time that we've applied the surcharge has been awesome. To be honest, the pushback has been minimal; 98 percent of guests are like, 'That's cool.'"[34]

ZFP created a variety of tools to help participating restaurants explain to their customers how the surcharge works and for public messaging with the media. Its tool kit included sample social media posts that chefs could personalize to show their support for the initiative, along with guidance on how to speak to the media. The team also worked with a public relations firm to generate op-eds and media stories. Outlets including *Eater*, *Bon Appétit*, the *New York Times*, and the *San Francisco Chronicle* were just a few of the media outlets featuring the campaign.

ZFP used this attention to further engage the restaurants in a policy advocacy push to get additional funding for the program from the state of California. The campaign included one-on-one meetings with the California secretary of agriculture, individual members of the California legislature, and the governor, Gavin Newsom. After several months, a collaboration agreement was put into place, and ZFP now works with several California state agencies to generate funding for farming practices that support a stable climate.

"We've always believed that restaurants could do more than serve food. The restaurant industry is by far the biggest sector in the food system at US$799 billion in the United States—larger than farming and retail. And more than just financial capital, I'd argue that chefs have the most cultural capital and agility as well," said Myint. "Zero Foodprint is all about redirecting a small fraction of that capital to help fund the transition toward regenerative agricultural practices."[35]

ZFP's campaign is globally recognized. The team won the Basque Culinary Food Prize and the James Beard Foundation's Humanitarian Award for their work. The initiative is also expanding. In 2022, ZFP became part of a multistate initiative working in California, Colorado, Georgia, and the Northeast United States. It is also working with chefs in Asia, Germany, and several Nordic countries.

"What ZFP does, what we recognized at the Beard Foundation, is they are making it easy for restaurants to get involved, helping the customers understand a pretty complex issue. ZFP also explains the urgency of the situation and delivers money directly to the farmers. They were smart communicators and made people stand up and pay attention. Their work will make a real difference for the planet," said Moon.[36]

Chapter 6

A Turning Point

We are all leaders. We're employers. We have a
certain level of public interest in our work. It is
important that we keep the pressure on. The industry
is still broken. The planet is dying. We need to act.
—Chef Preeti Mistry, chef,
activist, and author[1]

At some point in the summer of 2021, a friend and mentor asked me if I thought the time of the chef-activist was over. This question threw me into a bit of an existential crisis, but I knew exactly why it was asked: the COVID-19 pandemic had utterly upended the restaurant industry. For many chefs, saving their own restaurants—let alone saving the world—seemed impossible. Unless they were reaching out to members of Congress about hunger relief or financial support, chefs and restaurateurs were focused mostly on emergency feeding, supporting their staff, and keeping the doors of their businesses open.

Before the pandemic, efforts to get chefs a seat at the policy-making table were gaining steam. For years, we had been building an army of chef-advocates. They were working alongside the farmers, fishers, and other food advocates in an ongoing effort to change the policies, laws, and practices that control the food system. Chefs testified in front of Congress, spoke at the United Nations, and were working directly with governors and members of Congress across the United States. The community had big plans.

In the fall of 2019, nearly two hundred chefs gathered at Princeton University for the first-ever Chef Action Summit. There, they heard from speakers such as musician Questlove; Tracy K. Smith, United States poet laureate, 2017–2019; and Shannon Watts, founder of Moms Demand Action. Over the course of three days, chefs worked together to develop action plans related to the 2020 elections, including elevating the visibility of food during the upcoming presidential campaign. At the end of the summit, they were asked to make a commitment, articulating what issue they would work on, what types of activities they could host or participate in, and most importantly, how they were going to involve their staff, friends, and followers. Together, they committed to thousands of actions designed to raise awareness about the problems with our food system and generated dozens of thoughtful policy proposals they planned to submit to both political candidates and elected officials.

Until that time, we had made some strides in injecting food into the political discourse, but it was piecemeal. In 2016, the Chef Action Network and Food Policy Action (the group founded by Tom Colicchio) pushed for discussion of food in the presidential debates, and Food Policy Action published polling and developed a campaign focused on food and hunger issues in several congressional districts. Similar tactics were used in 2018. The 2020 elections presented a new opportunity for chefs to get involved at the highest level of policy-making.

I left Princeton buoyed by the idea that chefs were going to show up in a big way over the next year and that food would be a top point of discussion in the 2020 presidential election. The chefs were trained and ready. Their commitments ranged from hosting policy salons to helping with voter registration. For several months after the summit, our team at the James Beard Foundation mapped out timelines and activities. It was all coming together.

Then came March 2020.

When COVID-19 shut down the world, the restaurant industry was a frontline casualty of the pandemic. More than eleven million people were thrown out of work, the cyclical economy of restaurants ground to a halt, and experts called it an extinction-level event for the restaurant industry. Restaurants around the country started to close, and we pulled down every bit of in-person training and advocacy programming at the James Beard Foundation.

When it became clear that the pandemic wasn't something that would last only a few weeks, our team introduced online education and helped with the formation of the Independent Restaurant Coalition. Chefs used the training they had received at the Chef Bootcamp for Policy and Change to fight for restaurant aid and the money to help feed the tens of millions of newly food insecure Americans.

A few months later, after the brutal murder of George Floyd in May 2020, the long-simmering stew of wage discrepancies, sexual harassment, and racism boiled over as workers called out their employers and their actions, including the toxic behavior of celebrity chefs. Waiters and kitchen staffs, who had been deputized as health and mask monitors and were risking their lives going to work to feed unappreciative customers for subminimum wage, demanded accountability from owners, operators, investors, customers, and, again, chefs.

For once, the focus was on food workers and everything they endured to bring food to the table. A study from the University of California, San Francisco found that line cooks, bakers, and agriculture workers were among the professions to have the highest risk of mortality during the COVID pandemic—in some cases higher than even health care workers. According to the study, line cooks had a 60 percent increase in mortality associated with the pandemic.[2] Food system workers eligible for government benefits were using them more—and for longer. Those unable to collect unemployment or participate in the federal Supplemental Nutrition Assistance Program (SNAP), including the millions of undocumented immigrants who are the backbone of the industry, were forced to depend on GoFundMe campaigns and community feeding projects, some of which were housed in the restaurants where they worked.

As months went by, thousands of restaurants closed permanently, and those that remained open struggled with rising food costs, higher wage and benefit costs, and revenue losses. For almost three years, the pandemic killed both the businesses and the people needed to bring the industry back to life.

Throughout the pandemic, the idea of advocacy training for chefs felt quaint. The community had no capacity to expend energy on anything other than economic recovery and helping workers avoid hunger, eviction, illness, and death.

Everywhere I went, people seemed desperate for a return to so-called normal. I lost count of the number of calls and meetings I had with restaurant owners who were holding out hope that everything would go back to the way it was pre-COVID. I honestly still can't believe it. Normal wasn't working for our food system pre-COVID. Normal didn't save the lives of thousands of food workers who died during the pandemic. Normal didn't provide adequate wages or healthy work environments all along the food chain. If the restaurant industry goes back to what it was before, we will have thrown away a huge opportunity to do better for the planet and the people in our communities.

Chefs who choose normal will also be on the wrong side of the movement for a more fair, equitable, and sustainable food system. The world is changing, and you need to be part of those changes.

Never have we had such a clear picture of what the food system costs, who it supports, and pathways for changing it. Every restaurant owner who applied for emergency relief knows exactly how much it costs to pay their staff a fair wage (and one that makes up for lost tip revenue). Every chef better understands the financial costs and human toll of the food they serve. Policy makers and their staffs have more data about the benefits of social safety net programs such as universal school meals and emergency feeding programs. At one point, more than fifty-four million Americans were food insecure; the pandemic showed us all what happens when our supply chain collapses.[3]

If we squander these learnings, we will only have ourselves to blame. It is in our best interest, and our responsibility, to change both our own industry and the broader food system.

Cleaning Up Our Kitchens

As mentioned earlier, I was initially reluctant to work on advocacy with chefs because of the restaurant industry's internal failings. COVID-19 put those failings into sharp relief and also gave the industry a clear opportunity to begin cleaning up its own kitchen.

There's no better place to start than with wages. I understand that the cost of labor is one area that divides the restaurant community. Restaurant owners facing tight margins and the threat of shutting their doors are understandably nervous about one of their core costs going up. But given the industry's size and reach, the need to modernize wages and benefits simply can't be avoided.

According to the US Department of Labor, the restaurant industry is among the lowest-paying employers in the United States. As of 2023, the federal government allowed employers to pay workers who earn tips only $2.13 an hour (the federal minimum wage is currently $7.25). Although the actual minimum wage differs by state, forty-two states allow restaurants to take advantage of the subminimum wage.[4]

That was true when I waited tables as a teenager and college student in Florida. The federal wage was then $3.35, and

I took home less than $50 a week in employer-paid wages. Today the minimum wage in Florida is $10 an hour, but employers take a tip credit of $3.02 per hour, allowing them to pay tipped employees a wage of $6.98 per hour. Based on a thirty-five-hour week (to make sure workers don't qualify for full-time employee benefits), this wage amounts to less than $12,800 a year (the federal poverty line).[5]

In states with a subminimum wage, tipped restaurant workers are at least two times more likely to live in poverty than the general US population. The subminimum wage also exacerbates racial and gender pay disparities, as 40 percent of tipped workers are people of color and more than two-thirds are women.[6]

Some in the industry recognize this massive problem and are actively working to change it. For example, chef Amanda Cohen, who owns both Dirt Candy and Lekka Burger in New York City, was one of more than one hundred chefs and restaurateurs who signed a letter in 2018 urging then-governor Andrew Cuomo to eliminate the tipped minimum wage, along with other policies to help hospitality workers.[7] Cohen is one of the loudest and steadiest voices in the industry calling for changing wages.

She eliminated tipping in her restaurant as early as 2014, and in 2019, after New York approved a minimum wage increase, she wrote:

> I barely felt this minimum wage increase. I had to raise a few of my part-time prep workers from $15 an hour to $16 or $17 because suddenly everyone was paying their back of house $15 an hour, and I need to keep my pay rates competitive. But otherwise, my payroll barely budged. My

front-of-house workers already make between $25 and $30 an hour. My back-of-house team gets $17 to $20 an hour. I am an idiot for thinking the minimum wage is just that—the bare minimum. Why would I expect my employees to give me their best if I'm giving them the minimum? I also wonder how anyone who makes more than minimum wage feels comfortable eating in a restaurant that pays its employees minimum wage, but then again, I'm from Canada, and we're encouraged to think that way.[8]

For years, Cohen was one of a small group in this fight. As she explained, she believes that real change isn't going to happen if wage increases are voluntary:

It's almost impossible for restaurants to change one at a time. We need to change the whole system. But the NRA [National Restaurant Association] and others put out studies that tell a different story. They scare people into thinking a wage increase or benefits will destroy their businesses. It's simply not true. Yes, it's harder. Yes, it might cost more. But we must do better, be better businesspeople. It's the only way to truly be proud of our businesses and part of the community.[9]

Efforts to raise the minimum wage nationally, as well as to eliminate the tip credit, are being led by advocacy organizations including the Service Employees International Union, United Food and Commercial Workers, and the campaign One Fair Wage. These and other organizations are advocating for a raise in the federal minimum wage from $7.25 to at least $15 (or a livable wage, as advocates refer to it) and the complete elimination of the tip credit.

(The majority of the fifty US states, excluding Alaska, California, Guam, Minnesota, Montana, Nevada, Oregon, and Washington, allow tip credit—the reducing of a tipped employee's minimum wage to account for wages from customer-paid tips.)

Like Cohen, chef Renee Erickson of the Sea Creatures Restaurant Group in Seattle was at the forefront of the wage issue in 2016 when she eliminated tipping and increased the hourly wage for her employees. The reason, she said, came down to her values as a businesswoman: "We're a for-profit company, but we have other concerns that are important to us as well, and that is definitely our employees. We didn't want to be like other companies, often much bigger companies, where someone might have to work two or three jobs. We want our team to live the life they deserve."[10]

Building higher wages into a successful business model feels daunting for many restaurateurs. Higher wages often correspond with higher prices for customers, changes to hours and staffing structure, and even operational changes. Making these changes, and retaining and elevating employees, can be difficult. It's particularly hard when other restaurants don't have to follow the same rules, which is why chefs like Cohen and Erickson are pushing for policy change to create an even playing field. Yet, even with a concerted advocacy effort, convincing legislators, whether at the state or federal level, to raise the minimum wage is no easy feat. In the meantime, the chefs are showing that it is possible to pay fair wages while running a profitable business.

They are also part of a group of chefs that are standing up to efforts by the National Restaurant Association (NRA) to defeat increases in the minimum wage. The

NRA funds efforts at the state and local level to defeat any bills that would improve restaurant workers' wages, rights, and benefits. Funded in part by the wages of restaurant employees, the NRA spends approximately $3 million each year on lobbying expenses and donations to members of Congress.[11] In 2023, Senators Elizabeth Warren (D-MA) and Bernie Sanders (I-VT) even launched a congressional investigation into the NRA's use of fees required to be paid by workers for food safety training classes to "turn waiters and cooks into unwitting funders of its battle against minimum wage increases."[12]

Due to the NRA's work and that of other lobbyists, all efforts to raise the federal minimum wage have failed. But there has been progress on the state and local level. Nine states and the District of Columbia require employers to pay tipped workers the full state minimum wage, and advocacy efforts by groups such as One Fair Wage continue to push the issue to the forefront.

Tired of waiting for states to act and recognizing a need to do better by their employees, some owners and operators are looking for new ways to organize their businesses. Within the industry, interest is growing in unions, employee-owned cooperatives, and using financial incentives included in policy packages to help accelerate change.

One alternative business structure that's gaining traction is the Certified B Corporation. This distinction is held most frequently by giant food companies such as Amy's, Ben & Jerry's, and King Arthur Flour. Increasingly, restaurant and hospitality businesses are turning to this model to both distinguish themselves and ensure that they are doing right by their employees and communities. To become a

Certified B Corporation, a company's commitment to sustainable and equitable practices is assessed, and if the company scores high enough to achieve B Corp status, it becomes legally bound to "consider the impact of their decisions on their workers, customers, suppliers, community, and the environment."[13]

Tess Hart, co-owner and chief executive officer of Triple Bottom, a mission-driven brewery in Philadelphia, believes that the time and energy it took to have her business operations reviewed to attain B Corp status was worth it both for customers and employees. She explained, "Since I learned about B Corps, I have looked up to them . . . [as] a powerful symbol of a business that has really done the work . . . There is also the customer loyalty piece, which is much harder to quantify. And then I think our team is proud that we've achieved this. . . . Hiring people is expensive, training people is expensive, and if you can have a team that wants to see you thrive, that's huge."[14]

Becoming a B Corp takes time and financial resources. Today, though, Triple Bottom is just one of hundreds of food and beverage businesses around the United States making the switch to a model that focuses on the larger impacts of their operations.

Another way for restaurants to live their values and promote complete transparency with their staff is by adopting open-book management. In this system, everyone in the restaurant or business has the financial skills and literacy to take responsibility for the effective operation of the company. It requires a high level of business education and helps ensure that everyone knows their role in the business's success (or challenges).

Ari Weinzweig, cofounder of Zingerman's in Michigan, is a tireless advocate for open-book management. He explained:

> One of the critical elements of our principles is that we involve as many people as possible in running the business. And, in so doing, Zingerman's runs more effectively, benefiting from everyone's abilities, creativity, experience, and intelligence. We work to live this principle in every area of our organizational activity. All of our meetings are open. We involve front-line staff in interviewing and hiring. Our HR folks learn about merchandising. And our dishwashers learn about finance.
>
> The commitment from that level of involvement and influence is very, very high. People feel a meaningful part of something special regardless of seniority, title, age, or experience level. When it's working well, it's a pretty fantastic thing to see.[15]

The team at Zingerman's trains hundreds of owners and managers each year in their approach. Those who practice open-book finances find that their employees take on more responsibility while feeling more engaged and respected.

Both B Corp certification and open-book management are models that help restaurants put their philosophy on display. However, the employees are still working in service of the owner's vision and decisions.

Another model, the worker-owned cooperative, levels the playing field even more. Worker cooperatives are equally owned and governed by employees, who also earn money from the profits of their labor. In worker cooperatives, decision-making is democratic. Policies can't be decided by fiat; instead, each worker-owner has one vote. There are fewer than one hundred restaurants structured as cooperatives (out of about five hundred total cooperatives in the United States),[16] but the number is growing slowly.

The worker-owned model's biggest beneficiaries are traditionally marginalized workers, including the formerly incarcerated. Cooperatives increase opportunities to build credit and business acumen and help redistribute power across the industry. Nearly 60 percent of people employed at worker cooperatives identify as people of color, and more than 64 percent identify as women or nonbinary.[17] These worker-owners tend to be more supportive and open to policies and practices that aren't readily found in the industry, including paid sick leave, family leave, and continuing education.

The worker-owned cooperative model offers many benefits, especially for the industry's employees, said Devita Davison, executive director of Food Lab in Detroit. "When you own a part of the business, you have a greater degree of say over the kind of people in power. You're better able to control the conditions around you. When the workers own the business, they tend to pay themselves a decent wage and have better benefits."[18]

It's also better for staff retention, said Davison. "There is usually a lower staff turnover rate, a perennial, problematic issue in the restaurant industry."[19]

Chef-activist Reem Assil began the transition of her business to a worker-owned cooperative in 2021. Although she recognizes that hers is just one business, she hopes it will be a model for others. "You have to give real ownership and control in order to make it centered around the people who are impacted by this industry," she explained. "So, for us, obviously, success is the building of wealth, but also the building of leadership and a different way of doing things that become more normalized over time. It doesn't become the outlier—because Reem's being a worker-owned space doesn't really change the industry. It has to scale, and people have to follow suit."[20]

These efforts to change the restaurant industry's financial model are exciting, but will take time. They are not the only ones that the industry needs to make. For too long, the restaurant industry—and the greater food system—has limped along with a business culture that doesn't prioritize workers' health, safety, and well-being. In addition to addressing wages, the industry also needs to tackle health care, mental health, equity, and sexual harassment. These issues are some of the biggest challenges in our society, not just in the restaurant industry.

For reform to move beyond individual restaurants to the whole industry, chefs, restaurateurs, and workers must push for policy changes that raise wages and provide incentives to help stabilize businesses as they adopt new models. They will also have to stand up to the NRA and other lobbying groups. Doing so requires a methodical approach using the tactics we've discussed throughout this book.

From Politics to Policy

If COVID-19 forced the restaurant industry to look inward, it also showed the absolute necessity of looking beyond the four walls of an establishment. Bad policies failed to protect restaurant workers during the pandemic, but bad politics made a dire situation even worse. The toxic rhetoric that politicized social distancing, the wearing of masks, and vaccines pushed restaurant owners and workers to the frontlines, unprotected by inconsistent practices. The rhetoric around the pandemic reinforced the lesson that policy change ultimately depends on politicians taking stands. Sometimes, advocating for an issue also means advocating for a particular candidate. Advocacy can put us squarely into campaigns and partisan politics.

We had tried to avoid getting political at the Chef Action Network for years. In both our chef training and our advocacy, we stressed consensus building and were mostly nonpartisan—until we weren't.

In 2008, Aaron Tidman, a lawyer and food enthusiast, organized chefs to hold fundraisers for Barack Obama's first presidential campaign. Chefs for Obama raised hundreds of thousands of dollars for the campaign, and Tidman organized similar efforts in 2012. In 2016, when I met Tidman, the chefs' fundraising activities led them to get involved in voter education and registration efforts. Using the hashtags #votefood and #feedthevote, chefs worked for cycles to inject food policy into the debate and media discourse around the presidential and US Senate campaigns.

During the 2020 election cycle, as the pandemic raged, more than two dozen women chefs came together and organized voter registration efforts. They continued that work in the 2021 Senate runoff in Georgia to help elect Raphael Warnock. Using social media, including virtual cooking classes on Instagram and Facebook, these chefs helped get thousands of restaurant workers and customers to the polls (and helped feed the lines when voting took hours). These efforts paid off and opened new opportunities for chef-advocates to get involved in policy debates.

During his first weeks in office, Warnock joined the Senate Agriculture Committee and became a staunch supporter of programs for Black farmers and ranchers. Post-COVID, chefs, buoyed by their work on multiple campaigns and the rise of food policy, claimed a seat at the table with the US Department of Agriculture (USDA) on issues such as meat processing and funding for local food systems. They've also rejoined advocacy efforts focused on sustainable seafood and programs to end hunger and helped pass the first food waste reduction law in 2022.

Sponsors of the Food Donation and Improvement Act (FDIA) said that it will help get healthy, nutritious food to those who need it by strengthening liability protections for food businesses, including manufacturers, retailers, farmers, and restaurants that wish to donate surplus food. It also helps clarify existing guidance and best practices so that businesses can donate food safely and without the risk of litigation.[21] (The possibility of being sued if someone got sick after eating food donated to food banks and shelters was a huge concern of chefs and restaurants, and FDIA addresses those fears.)

Chef-advocate Colicchio said that by wasting food, "we're devaluing not just the food, but we're devaluing the people who are responsible for feeding us."[22] For just over a year, he and other chef-advocates met with members of Congress, published op-eds, attended meetings with the USDA and the Biden administration, and urged their fans and followers on social media to learn more about FDIA and call their members of Congress. The momentum started by chefs like

Steven Satterfield, Mourad Lahlou, and Tiffany Derry in 2016 helped lay the groundwork for the work in 2022 (see chapter 2). Activists delivered messages of support for the bill from all fifty states and met in Washington, DC, for a day of action in the spring of 2022. The bill passed with bipartisan support, and the president signed FDIA into law on January 5, 2023. This new law will help reduce the amount of food that goes unsold or uneaten in the United States and reduce hunger for more than forty-two million.[23]

By helping secure policy wins like FDIA, chefs, farmers, and small business owners continue to demonstrate their relevancy to policy debates at the highest levels. As chef Mary Sue Milliken said, "I think we have a lot of opportunities to talk more about our food system than ever before. Our relationships with members of Congress are stronger. They know us now. We have to use our experiences lobbying for restaurant aid to inform how we show up for other groups and fight for food as a human right."[24]

The Fight Is Global

Chefs are not only stepping up to the challenges in the restaurant industry and in US policy, but also to those that affect the entire planet. After all, the problems in the US food system are present in nearly every country around the world. According to the United Nations, the global population is expected to grow to more than ten billion by 2040.[25] From country governments to food companies to local food banks, everyone is looking for a way to both feed people and tackle the consistent strains that food production puts on the environment. In September 2021, the

United Nations hosted the first global food summit where thousands of representatives from member countries, global companies, and food tech startups joined experts, scientists, and advocates from around the world to discuss the food system's problems. Among the groups represented was the Chefs' Manifesto.

Created and managed by Paul Newnham, the Chefs' Manifesto is a loose collective of more than one thousand chefs from ninety countries advocating for countries to commit resources to the United Nations Sustainable Development Goals, especially efforts to "end hunger, achieve food security and improved nutrition, and promote sustainable agriculture by 2030."[26]

Chef William Dissen, who is a member of the Chefs Diplomatic Corps and who works with both the US State Department and Chefs' Manifesto, believes that food is central to discussions around climate change. "It's been amazing to be part of a global community of chefs and farmers who are interested in how we change the food system," he said. "Meeting people, sitting in on those conversations, exploring other fields and fisheries, I've gotten a chance to think about how we are connected. I then bring that home to conversations with my members of Congress about everything from fisheries management to the Farm Bill to hunger. And we aren't just talking but also looking for solutions."[27]

One of the solutions is money. The United States contributes approximately $3 billion each year to the United Nations World Food Programme (WFP), which provides emergency food relief and runs programs to help reduce food insecurity around the world.

Some experts expect the number of food insecure people around the world to continue to rise due to the impacts of climate change, global conflicts, and economic challenges faced by every country, from Brazil to Nigeria. These global challenges require a global response, but the United States plays a key role in funding emergency feeding and food production worldwide.

This funding is part of the annual federal budget, and every year, opponents of the United Nations try to remove the money. This pushback on funding demands a coordinated response from supporters of WFP's work, including chefs who meet regularly with members of Congress and their staffs.

To raise awareness about the importance of the United States's contribution to WFP's funding, both in Congress and with the US media, chef and TV personality Andrew Zimmern became a goodwill ambassador for the agency in 2021. At the time of the announcement, he said, "A healthy and remade food system is within our grasp and because we are enduring a global existential climate crisis, we have a clock running down that is making that work even more challenging. We have the skill set needed to feed a hungry planet, yet many countries lack the will or resources to see the job through. The WFP is working diligently around the world on real, lasting solutions and I am honored to assist them."[28]

International efforts are complemented by the work of chefs in individual countries outside the United States. For instance, the tremendous efforts by Satterfield, Lahlou, and Derry to reduce food waste in the United States have counterparts around the globe. For a number of years, I worked with chefs in Australia, another country where food waste is a major problem. In 2019, Australia wasted more food than even the United States.[29]

Chef Kylie Kwong, who has hundreds of thousands of social media followers, uses her public platform to bring awareness to the connection between food waste and climate change. In an interview with *Foodwise*, Kwong explained that rotting food in landfills produces methane, a potent greenhouse gas. She went on to explain her personal commitment to the issue: "If we're serious about tackling climate change and creating a safer future for Australia's children, then we need to do everything possible to reduce the amount of food that we use and throw out. . . . It is not only the contribution that my staff and I want to make to the community, it is actually our duty, as I see it, for after all, we humans are simply 'caretakers of this planet.'"[30]

Chefs Are Persistent

A trait I appreciate in any advocate is persistence, especially in the face of nearly impossible odds and challenging circumstances. It is a characteristic I think those who work in restaurants, hospitality, and in the food world have in excess. You never give up—even when sometimes you need to stop and regroup. This community of people is tenacious. To keep a farm going for generations or open a new restaurant during a global pandemic or recession, you have to be.

There is one more topic that comes up where I think that chefs and restaurateurs can and should bring that persistence in support of policy change: gun control. Yes, I used the words *gun control*. Gun violence is past the point of crisis in the United States. According to the nonpartisan advocacy group Everytown for Gun Safety, between 2015 and 2022, more than nineteen thousand people were shot and killed or wounded in the United States in a mass shooting.[31] In 2021, the Federal Bureau of Investigation ranked restaurants as the eighth most common location for violent crime, including seventy-six murders.[32]

This problem isn't new. In 1991, a mass shooting took place at a Luby's Cafeteria in Killeen, Texas, where twenty-three people were killed (plus the perpetrator) and another twenty-seven wounded. Other restaurants and clubs have been the site of horrific shootings, including Pulse Nightclub in Orlando, Florida, and Colonel Brooks Tavern in Washington, DC.

Yet, the restaurant industry has largely sat the debate out. In 2020, executives from more than 140 companies sent a letter to the US Senate urging the passage of legislation that included a background check on all gun purchasers. Not a single restaurant chief executive officer, nor the leaders of the National Restaurant Association, signed the letter. Despite the violence directed at restaurant employees and the challenges chefs and owners face from the myriad different laws, the industry lobby did nothing to protect itself or its workers.

That's not to say that chefs and restaurateurs aren't doing something. National chain restaurants such as Starbucks, Chili's, Chipotle, and Panera Bread each have policies that ask customers not to openly carry weapons into their locations (regardless of whether state laws might allow it). A few states—Maine, Louisiana, North Dakota, and Illinois—completely ban guns in restaurants. Chefs in cities around the country, including *Top Chef* contestant

Carl Dooley in Boston, have worked with Moms Demand Action to raise money and awareness about efforts to end gun violence and build safer communities. And, in some cases, chefs in states where the open carry of a firearm is permitted, have posted signs prohibiting customers from bringing a gun into their restaurants.

This position isn't easy or popular, and in some cases, it can incite threats and boycotts against restaurants that take a stand against gun violence. It is, however, a place where, as business owners and community leaders, chefs can make a difference, even if it's one step at a time.

As one chef told me after the February 2023 mass shooting at Michigan State University, "People don't need their gun to enjoy a meal. We want everyone to feel safe. So, we now post signs saying no guns are allowed. It's small, but it is a start."[33] Dooley, the chef from Boston, told *Forbes* at the time of his fundraiser, "We have a collective responsibility as parents to make our kids safe. I never thought about being shot in school, and it is something that kids and teachers are trained in. How frightening is that? I'm not anti-gun. We just need to do a better job in society to keep our children safe."[34]

Your Seat at the Table Is Waiting

Keeping our kids safe. Protecting our staffs. Combating climate change. Making sure everyone has food on the table. Chefs are at work on all these issues—and more. It is a lot. Claiming your seat at the table with policy makers in the United States and around the world can feel daunting. After all, our relationship to food is complicated, deeply personal, and very political (whether we know it or not). I don't think I've ever heard the words *love* and *hate* more than I have when working in food. Our personal tastes, our cultures and life experiences, and our access to different foods make each of us a critic, and not always generous. Yet generosity is exactly what chefs require, both in running your restaurant and becoming an effective advocate.

Despite the challenges of the last few years, chefs, restaurateurs, and food workers are still some of the best champions for a new food system. Restaurants are one of our primary economic hubs, both regionally and nationally. Millions of Americans get their start—and build lasting careers—in the food and hospitality industry. Few groups are as intricately connected to the people who produce our food and the people who make the laws that control our system as chefs. Remaking our food system will require everyone to do their part and step up to lead.

On the last day of every advocacy training, I ask participants to commit themselves to work on an issue once they leave. Each participant must answer three questions:

1. What's the first thing you will do with the training and information you received?
2. What is the issue or challenge you most want to work on?
3. What do you want to accomplish in the next year on this issue?

In the early days of the Chef Bootcamp for Policy and Change, we asked every participant to fill out a postcard and address it to themselves, and we mailed the postcards to the participants later in the year. In later boot camps, we asked chefs to write their commitments on large sticky notes and present them to one another before leaving for the airport. Either way, the chefs committed to using their voice, their networks, and their platform to create real change.

Regardless of their particular issue or on how they moved forward, these chefs are now among the most respected and active advocates for a better food system. Together, they've accelerated changes in federal policy, set up organizations to tackle mental health challenges, committed the industry to address racism, championed farmworker rights, and helped push for a more sustainable food system for both people and the planet.

Early in 2018, at the James Beard Foundation Awards in Chicago, chef Dominique Crenn won for Best Chef: West. During her acceptance speech, she said, "I rise in support of equality, humanity, and Mother Earth."[35] That same night, chef José Andrés of World Central Kitchen received the Humanitarian of the Year Award, and he urged the audience to "see the world's greatest challenges not as problems but as opportunities for us to serve." As he explained, "Hunger, poverty, environmental destruction, equal treatment of women in the workplace, immigration reform for the millions of hard-working immigrants who feed America and make our country great, especially the Dreamers and the eleven million undocumented who deserve to be part of the American dream—these issues seem very different, but they are all connected. Food touches everything."[36]

Hundreds of thousands of people watched their speeches live via social media. Inside Chicago's Lyric Theater, thousands of chefs, restaurateurs, and hospitality workers heard

the calls for the industry to stand up for more than delicious food. As Andrés closed his speech, he called for
everyone in the room to be part of a movement to change
the world, saying, "It's not about me the person, it's about
we the people . . . and we can improve the world, one plate
at a time."[37] The audience rose for a standing ovation. For
everyone who worked on the Chef Bootcamp for Policy
and Change, those speeches also validated a journey we
had started in 2012 to change how the food world saw
chefs and how they saw themselves.

Right after the awards presentation that year, I accompanied a group of chefs, farmers, and small business owners traveling to Washington, DC, to meet with members
of Congress about the 2018 Farm Bill. That bill included
several priorities supported by the chef community, such as
food waste reduction projects and grants to provide more
fruits and vegetables for SNAP recipients. This work was just
one piece of what was happening around the country—and
world. From hyperlocal events to international advocacy,
we saw chefs sitting at the table for policy change.

Today, chefs are working with leaders in other
fields—from urban farmers to social justice organizers to
community activists—to achieve a better food system for
all. These efforts take many forms, but they all share a common DNA—the belief that chefs can make a difference.

Many of those stories are shared in this book, but there
are so many more efforts to highlight. Chef Hari Pulapaka
of Cress in Deland, Florida, is a tireless champion for the
rights and voice of immigrants. He was a founding board
member of the Chef Action Network and a go-to resource
for chefs thinking about getting into policy advocacy. He's

spoken to members of Congress about the labeling of genetically modified foods, sustainable seafood, and child nutrition. Together with his co-owner and partner, Jenneffer Pulapaka, he organized a coalition of chefs focused on economic development policies in South Florida. In the thick of the debate about the Muslim travel ban, he hosted a citywide dinner to raise awareness of immigration policies.

Chef Mario Pagán stood alongside Andrés's World Central Kitchen in Puerto Rico to provide millions of meals for US citizens left without food or resources there after Hurricane Maria stormed through the Caribbean in 2017, and he continues to serve as an advocate for the island. Hundreds of chefs are now part of World Central Kitchen's Chefs Corps, and they've worked across the world, including during the war in Ukraine starting in 2022.

Chefs Abra Berens, Ben Hall, Dejuan Roy, and Tiffany Derry meet regularly with lawmakers and their staffs about funding to promote small farmers and support for transitioning farmers to more environmentally friendly practices. There are hundreds of stories to tell, and a lot of progress has been made. Things are getting better.

It isn't all inspirational and sunny, but when I think of these chefs and all the community has achieved over the years, it gives me hope. That's why when my friend and mentor asked me if this industry, with all its problems, could still advocate for change, I said yes. Chefs can and should be a voice for good in this complicated system. You know how to get it done. Now get to work.

Acknowledgments

First, I want to thank the thousands of chefs, restaurateurs, farmers, and food activists who went through at least one of the pieces of the "A Is for Advocacy" training at the James Beard Foundation's Chef Bootcamp for Policy and Change, Chef Action Network (CAN) regional boot camps, and policy salons and other trainings.

From the first pilot in 2012 to my last Chef Bootcamp in the fall of 2020, working with you was simply amazing. You taught me much about the food system and introduced me to many other chefs, producers, and thinkers. You asked all the right, and tough, questions. Then, you took what you learned and put it into action. Because of you, we know that what's laid out in this book works.

You know who you are and how much I appreciate all you do to make the world a better place. I'm incredibly grateful for every late-night firepit conversation, for every time you took the time to call a member of Congress, for each moment you made the decision to use your voice. You took training tools and techniques I had learned and taught around the globe and helped turn them into something relevant to chefs and others in the food world. Thank you for helping perfect this recipe for change and for putting it into action.

Now, I hope this book inspires other chefs to get into the fight for a better food system.

For some, including many who are highlighted in the chapters themselves, advocacy is a now way of life. I'm in awe of you all but am especially grateful for those I met in the early days, including Hugh Acheson, Charleen Badman, Abra Berens, Tiffany Derry, William Dissen, Renee Erickson, Duskie Estes, Ben Hall, Maria Hines, Phil Jones, Ed Kenney, Spike Mendelsohn, Preeti Mistry, Patrick Mulvaney, Hari Pulapaka, and Andrea Reusing. Thank you for always making time for me. Thank you for being good humans and knowing how to get shit done.

There wouldn't be a book—or even a field of chef advocacy—without Eric Kessler and chef Michel Nischan. Together, they had the vision for Chef Bootcamp for Policy and Change and CAN. Their idea, energy, personal and political will, and creativity brought me into the fold. They gave me the keys to a world that I didn't know existed before and changed my life forever. They also constantly champion the belief that food policy is smart policy and that chefs should have a seat at that table. President Kristopher Moon, trustees Emily Luchetti and Mary Sue Milliken, and Mitchell Davis, past senior vice president of strategy, were the strongest advocates for the program at the James Beard Foundation. Funding from philanthropists Samantha Campbell, Chris and Meredith Powell, and the Waitt Foundation helped us keep the programming going in the early days. There are many others, but two Beard staff members, Ashley Kosiak and Maggie Schoenfarber, helped organize and then promote most of the Chef Bootcamps. I'm also indebted to Alexina Cather, Patricia Griffin, and

Anne McBride, who continued to train chefs using much of this curriculum even after I left the foundation.

Nothing about this book was easy, and it wouldn't have happened without the kindness, expertise, and creativity of Emily Turner. From the first phone call exploring the idea to the last minutes of production, she held my hand and made *At the Table* a much better book than it was a training curriculum, which is saying a lot.

Dozens of people read drafts of this book, including Brent Colburn, Jill Colgan, Matt Erickson, Terence Samuel, Andrew Solomon, and Sujata Tejwani. After reading so many versions, I'm so glad they are still my friends. A special thanks to Sujata, who worked with me on the Chef Bootcamp curriculum in the early days and during the pandemic. She is one of the best trainers and coaches in the world, and every moment of her time is a gift.

I met my husband, Lou, during the first days of the Chef Bootcamp and the creation of the Chef Action Network. He allowed our kitchen table to be taken over by training materials, traveled with me around the country, and held my hand throughout the building of the programs, the writing of this book, and every milestone along the way. The same is true of some of my dearest friends, including Annie Brown, Amy Dacey, Natasha Stott Despoja, Christine Elliott, Sarah Gesiriech, Stephanie Cohen Glass, Trish Hoppey, Karen Rosen, and Claire Thwaites. They show up in big and small ways in my life, and I love them all.

Finally, I'm grateful and blessed to have been raised by a group of women—from my grandmother to my aunts—who encouraged me to travel, write, and pursue a body of work even when they didn't understand it or even know where in the world I was on any given day. Thank you to my aunt Anna Strickland and, most especially, my mom, Janis Gemignani, for asking the tough questions but always being my strongest supporters.

Back in the early days of this work, a quote from James Beard was uncovered: "If we really believe in food, we must do something about it, for our voices should be raised above the rest." My thanks to everyone who believes that, puts it into practice, and changes the world a little at a time, every day.

Appendix

Advocacy Organizations You Should Know

In recent years, dozens of nonprofit organizations and advocacy groups have developed specific programs to support chefs in your advocacy work. Below are organizations that work directly with the chef community to advocate for sourcing, industry operations, and policy changes. All the information listed here is taken from the organizations' websites. Please reach out to these groups directly to learn more. I keep an updated version of this list on my website, www.table81.com.

National

Bakers Against Racism. Bakers Against Racism was founded as a social community, connecting bakers and creatives all across the globe to fight against racism in all its forms. Since activating Bakers Against Racism, more than three thousand people from more than two hundred US cities, more than forty US states, and five continents have participated in one of its global bake sales. https://www.bakersagainstracism.com/

BIPOC Foodways Alliance. Founded by journalist Mecca Bos and chef Sean Sherman, BIPOC Foodways

Alliance researches, archives, uplifts, and shares diverse food stories of all BIPOC communities in a changing United States. https://www.bipocfoodways.org/

Chefs for Healthy Soil. Chefs for Healthy Soil is a community of chefs across the United States who are part of a regenerative agriculture movement to support transformative food and agriculture policies. Their involvement also helps educate lawmakers, the media, and consumers about the inextricable link between soil health, food quality, and climate change. https://www.nrdc.org/chefs-healthy-soil/

Chefs Stopping AAPI Hate. Founded by chefs Tim Ma and Kevin Tien, Chefs Stopping AAPI Hate is an organization bringing together the culinary world to support Asian American and Pacific Islander (AAPI) and social justice causes. It originated in the spring of 2021 as a way to raise money and awareness of the increase in violence against Asian Americans in the United States. https://www.chefsstoppingaapihate.com/

Common Threads. Chef Art Smith cofounded Common Threads in 2003 to educate children on cooking and nutrition education, cultural diversity, and physical health and wellness. Common Threads takes an innovative approach to providing children, educators, caregivers, and health-care professionals with the resources, curriculum, and chef-led training needed to champion healthy cooking and nutrition education within their communities. https://www.commonthreads.org/

High Road Restaurants. High Road Restaurants advocates for fair wages and increased racial and gender equity through hiring, training, and promotional practices. https://highroadrestaurants.org/

Independent Restaurant Coalition (IRC). The restaurant and bar community formed the IRC to save the independent restaurants and bars, and the eleven million people they employ—and the five million workers up and down the supply chain—who are affected by COVID-19. The IRC was founded on the simple belief that small businesses have the power to affect legislative change. https://www.independentrestaurantcoalition.com/

James Beard Foundation. Chef advocacy is an important arm of the James Beard Foundation. Its Chef Bootcamp for Policy and Change was created in 2012 and is the foundation of its ongoing industry advocacy programs. https://www.jamesbeard.org/advocacy/

The National Black Food and Justice Alliance (NBFJA). NBFJA is a coalition of Black-led organizations advancing Black-led visions for just and sustainable communities and building capacity for self-determination within local, national, and international food systems and land rights work. https://www.blackfoodjustice.org/

North American Traditional Indigenous Food Systems (NATIFS) and Indigenous Food Lab (IFL). NATIFS and IFL are nonprofit organizations founded in part by James Beard Award winner chef Sean Sherman and the team at The Sioux Chef. NATIFS is dedicated to addressing the economic and health crises affecting Native communities by reestablishing Native foodways. IFL is an education and training center. https://www.natifs.org/

Regarding Her Food. Regarding Her Food (or RE:Her) is a national nonprofit organization on a mission to advance women-identifying and nonbinary food and beverage entrepreneurs and leaders by way of innovative platforms that include business, community, and advocacy opportunities. https://www.regardingherfood.com/

Studio ATAO. Founded by chef Jenny Dorsey, Studio ATAO stands for "all together at once." The group mission includes creating accessible, relevant resources that inspire socially conscious food, beverage, and hospitality professionals toward action through publicly available social justice education, vulnerable conversations, and community building. https://www.studioatao.org/

Wholesome Wave. Founded in 2007 by chef Michel Nischan, the late Gus Schumacher, and the late Michael Batterberry, Wholesome Wave was created to address diet-related diseases by helping low-income Americans buy and eat healthy fruits and vegetables. https://www.wholesomewave.org/

Zero Foodprint (ZFP). ZFP is a nonprofit organization mobilizing the food world around agricultural climate solutions. Named "Humanitarian of the Year" by the James Beard Foundation, ZFP sees the food system as a major solution to global warming as well as a major cause. ZFP members crowd-fund grants for farmers to switch to renewable farming practices—proven to be the most impactful initiative yet toward solving global warming. https://www.zerofoodprint.org/about/

International

CARE Chef's Table. Since 2014, CARE has worked with socially conscious chefs interested in influencing US policy makers and advancing CARE's international food security policies. Chefs Asha Gomez, Carla Hall, Matthew McClure, Spike Mendelsohn, and Judi Ni are among

the chefs listed as participating. https://www.care.org/get
-involved/join/chefs-table/

The Chefs' Manifesto. The Chefs' Manifesto is a chef-
led project that brings together more than eleven hundred
chefs from around the world to explore how they can help
deliver a sustainable food system. As chefs bridge the gap
between farm and fork, the Chefs' Manifesto empowers
chefs with a framework tied to the United Nations Sustainable Development Goals. https://sdg2advocacyhub
.org/chefs-manifesto/aboutus/

Culinary Diplomacy Project. The Culinary Diplomacy
Project is a chef-driven nonprofit organization that sends
prominent chefs to destinations around the world as representatives of American culture and cuisine. Following
each international trip, the chefs engage with American
audiences around the United States by participating in
events designed to share their experiences. https://www
.culinarydiplomacyproject.org/

Restaurant Workers' Community Foundation.
Restaurant Workers' Community Foundation raises and
distributes funds to grow the power of workers in public discourse and workplace policies on wages, equity, and
health by engaging in community building, advocacy,
grantmaking, network building, and impact investing.
https://www.restaurantworkerscf.org/

World Central Kitchen (WCK). WCK uses the power
of food to nourish communities and strengthen economies in times of crisis and beyond. When disaster strikes,
WCK's Chef Relief Team mobilizes to the front lines with
the urgency of now to start cooking and provide meals to
people in need. https://wck.org/

In the United States

Arizona

Blue Watermelon Project. Blue Watermelon Project, established in 2016, is a group of chefs, restaurateurs, farmers, and community food advocates who work together in a collective and committed effort to expand, encourage, and educate students to develop healthy relationships with food. Founded by chef Charleen Badman, the group works in twenty-four schools in Arizona and involves more than thirty chefs from around the state. https://www.bluewatermelonproject.org/

California

Bay Area Ranchers' Co-Op (BAR-C). BAR-C was founded to provide farming and ranching communities in the greater Bay Area with USDA-inspected animal harvest in a sustainable, noncompetitive environment. Chef Duskie Estes is a founding member. https://bayarearanchers.com/

Edible Schoolyard Project. The Edible Schoolyard Project is a nonprofit organization dedicated to the transformation of public education by using organic school gardens, kitchens, and cafeterias to teach both academic subjects and the values of nourishment, stewardship, and community. https://edibleschoolyard.org/

La Cocina. La Cocina is a nonprofit organization working to solve problems of equity in business ownership for women, immigrants, and people of color. Chef Reem Assil is an alumnus of La Cocina's programs. https://lacocinasf.org/

Colorado

The Chef Ann Foundation. The Chef Ann Foundation is dedicated to promoting whole-ingredient scratch cooking in schools. This approach enables schools to serve the healthiest, tastiest meals so that kids are well fed and ready to learn. Founded by chef Ann Cooper, the foundation champions school food reform as a way to improve childhood nutrition. https://www.chefannfoundation.org/

Connecticut

Brigaid. Chef Dan Giusti founded Brigaid in 2016. This national nonprofit organization places professional chefs in school kitchens to help cafeteria lunch staff cook up delicious, nourishing meals for kids. Brigaid also works with institutions of all types and sizes to help make demonstrable changes to their food service programs. https://www.chefsbrigaid.com/

Georgia

The Giving Kitchen. The Giving Kitchen is a nonprofit organization that helps food service workers in crisis. It provides stability through referrals to a network of low- or no-cost community resources. Food service workers who have experienced an injury, illness, housing disaster, or death of a family member can also receive financial assistance to cover living expenses. https://thegivingkitchen.org/

Illinois

Pilot Light. Pilot Light is a nonprofit organization founded by some of Chicago's top chefs to bring food education to students in Chicago Public Schools and help children make healthier choices. Chefs involved include Paul Kahan, Matthew Merges, and Beverly Kim. https://pilotlightchefs.org/

Massachusetts

Root. Root's mission is to help young adults create a pathway to independence through food service training and employment. By developing essential life and work readiness skills, youth leave Root prepared for success in the workplace. https://rootns.org/

New York

City Harvest. City Harvest is New York City's largest food rescue organization, helping to feed the nearly 1.2 million New Yorkers who are struggling to put meals on their tables. Its programs help food-insecure New Yorkers access nutritious food that fits their needs and desires and strengthen the local food system, building a path to a food-secure future for all New Yorkers. Michael Anthony, Dominique Ansel, Dan Barber, Emma Bengtsson, David Chang, Andrew Carmellini, Tom Colicchio, Dan Churchill, Michael Chernow, Lena Ciardullo, Scott Conant, Suzanne Cupps, Marc Forgione, Danny Meyer, and many other chefs are involved. https://www.cityharvest.org/

Pennsylvania

Vetri Community Partnership. Established by chef Marc Vetri to help kids experience the connection between healthy eating and healthy living, Vetri Community Partnership empowers children and families to lead healthier lives through fresh food, hands-on experiences, and education. https://vetricommunity.org/

Texas

I'll Have What She's Having. I'll Have What She's Having is an organization uniting women chefs, hospitality professionals, entrepreneurs, physicians, scientists, artists, and other professionals in social activism. It is focused on raising community awareness and funds in support of women's health. https://www.illhavewhatsheshaving.org/

Southern Smoke Foundation. Southern Smoke Foundation is a nonprofit organization launched by chef Chris Shepherd that has donated $1.3 million to "take care of our own" and more than $700,000 to the National Multiple Sclerosis Society (in honor of Shepherd's friend and former sommelier, Antonio Gianola, who was diagnosed with the disease). In addition, Southern Smoke's Emergency Relief Fund has donated more than $700,000 to industry professionals in crisis, helping out through natural disasters, health issues, and mental health issues. https://southernsmoke.org/

Notes

Chapter 1

1. Kwame Onwuachi, interview by author on Zoom, January 18, 2022.

2. Federal Food and Drug Administration, "GMO Crops, Animal Food, and Beyond," accessed February 11, 2023 (content current as of August 3, 2022), https://www.fda.gov/food/agricultural-biotechnology/gmo-crops-animal-food-and-beyond.

3. Eva Maria Hanson, "Which Agency Enforces Food Safety in a Restaurant or a Food Service Operation?," FoodDocs.com, September 16, 2022, https://www.fooddocs.com/post/which-agency-enforces-food-safety-in-a-restaurant.

4. WTMJ-Milwaukee, "Only 33 Percent of Restaurant Majority Owners Are Women," March 1, 2018, https://www.tmj4.com/news/local-news/only-33-percent-of-restaurant-majority-owners-are-women.

5. National Restaurant Association, "National Restaurant Association Outlines Concerns with Passage of Health Care Bill in U.S. House," press release, March 21, 2010.

6. NPR Staff, "For Tipped Workers, a Different Minimum Wage Battle," *All Things Considered*, NPR, June 29, 2014.

7. Jessica Reimer and Sarah Zorn, "What Is the Average Restaurant Profit Margin? Tips for Benchmarking and Optimizing," Toast Tab, last accessed April 27, 2023, https://pos.toasttab.com/blog/on-the-line/average-restaurant-profit-margin.

8. Brent Barnhart, "41 of the Most Important Social Media Marketing Statistics for 2022," Sprout Social, March 22,

2022, https://sproutsocial.com/insights/social-media
-statistics/.

9. Alexa Peduzzi, "Which Social Media Platform Should You
Use to Promote Your Food Blog?," *Foodbloggerpro*, November 11, 2020, https://www.foodbloggerpro.com/blog/social
-media-promote-food-blog/.

10. Marketing Charts, "8 in 10 US Adults Watch Cooking
Shows," August 2, 2010, https://www.marketingcharts.com/
television-13719#:~:text=Half%20of%20Americans%20
Watch%20Cooking%20Shows%20Occasionally%20or%20
More&text=More%20than%20half%20(55%25),or%20never
%20watch%20these%20shows.

11. Food Network (website), "About FoodNetwork.com," accessed February 12, 2023, https://www.foodnetwork.com/
site/about-foodnetwork-com.

12. Peter Hailey, "How Guy Fieri's Giant New TV Contract Would Stack Up in NFL," *Sports Washington*, NBC,
May 26, 2021, https://www.nbcsports.com/washington/
football-team/heres-how-guy-fieris-enormous-new-tv
-contract-would-stack-nfl.

13. Andrea Reusing, interview by author on Zoom, January 31,
2022.

14. Patrick Canning, Food Economics Division, Economic
Research Service, "Where Do Americans' Food Dollars
Go?" (blog), USDA, Research and Science, May 14, 2019,
https://www.usda.gov/media/blog/2019/05/14/where-do
-americans-food-dollars-go.

15. Eric Amel et al., "Independent Restaurants Are a Nexus of Small Businesses in the United States and Drive
Billions of Dollars of Economic Activity that Is at Risk
of Being Lost due to the Covid-19 Pandemic," Compass
Lexecon-Independent Restaurant Coalition White Paper,
June 10, 2020, https://media-cdn.getbento.com/accounts/

cf190ba55959ba5052ae23ba6d98e6de/media/R903wxAIRJG
ukLxai2ZB_Report.pdf.

16. Amel et al., "Independent Restaurants."

17. Jonathan Maize, "Restaurants Cut Jobs Last Month as Coronavirus Surges Again," *Restaurant Business*, September 2, 2021, https://www.restaurantbusinessonline.com/financing/restaurants-cut-jobs-last-month-coronavirus-surges-again.

18. National Restaurant Association, "2022 State of Restaurant Industry," February 9, 2022, https://restaurant.org/nra/media/research/reports/2022/soi2022-summary.pdf.

19. Ashira Prossack, "5 Traits of Highly Connected People," *Forbes*, December 28, 2018, https://www.forbes.com/sites/ashiraprossack1/2018/12/28/highly-connected-people-traits-networking/?sh=7feedb315e66.

20. Jamilka Borges, as told to author, September 2020.

21. Asha Gomez, in conversation with author, April 22, 2016.

22. Renee Erickson, interview by author on Zoom, March 30, 2022.

23. Michael Bartiromo, "Is It Illegal to Hand Out Water or Food Outside Your Polling Place?," *The Hill*, November, 1, 2022, https://thehill.com/homenews/nexstar_media_wire/3709676-is-it-illegal-to-hand-out-water-or-food-outside-your-polling-place/.

24. Mandi Wright, "Kamala Harris Stops in Detroit Ahead of Debate," July 29, 2019, *Detroit Free Press*, https://www.freep.com/picture-gallery/news/local/michigan/detroit/2019/07/29/kamala-harris-stops-detroit-ahead-debate/1859374001/.

25. Brittany Valentine, "VP Kamala Harris, Rep. Nanette Barragán Host D.C. Latina Business Leaders at the White House," *Al Dia*, September 30, 2021, https://aldianews.com/en/politics/policy/vp-harris-meets-latinas.

26. "2022 Edelman Trust Barometer: Food and Beverage," Edelman, accessed February 12, 2023, https://www.edelman.com/trust/2022-trust-barometer/food-beverage (last).

27. Center for Food Integrity, "A Clear View of Transparency and How It Builds Consumer Trust," January 2015.

28. Reusing, interview.

29. US Department of Agriculture, Food and Nutrition Service, SNAP Data Tables, accessed February 2023, https://www.fns.usda.gov/pd/supplemental-nutrition-assistance-program-snap.

30. Elle Simone, as told to author, February 2020.

31. Catalyst Trend Brief, "CEO Activism," February 21, 2021, https://www.catalyst.org/research/ceo-activism-trend-brief/.

32. Julie Kelly, "Tom Colicchio's Overcooked Politics," *Wall Street Journal*, October 29, 2014, https://www.wsj.com/articles/julie-kelly-tom-colicchios-overcooked-politics-1414621705.

33. Loi Azim, "Chefs Who Won't Just Shut Up and Cook," *Edible Manhattan*, August 17, 2016, https://www.ediblemanhattan.com/uncategorized/we-wont-just-shut-up-and-cook-chefs-join-the-fight-against-hunger/.

34. Ashley Christensen, as told to author, November 2016.

35. Debbie Shore, as told to author, November 2016.

36. Reusing, interview.

Chapter 2

1. Sue Bette, as told to author, December 2020.

2. Vermont Law School Center for Agriculture and Food Systems and Harvard Law School Food Law and Policy Clinic, "Blueprint for a National Food Strategy," February 2017, https://foodstrategyblueprint.org/wp-content/uploads/2017/03/Food-Strategy-Blueprint.pdf.

3. Doug Farquhar, National Council of State Legislatures, March 20, 2020, https://www.afdo.org/wp-content/uploads/2020/09/Food-Legislation-2019.pdf.

4. Agency Profile for United States Department of Agriculture, Center for Responsive Politics, accessed February 13, 2023, https://www.opensecrets.org/federal-lobbying/agencies/summary?cycle=2019&id=023.

5. National Sustainable Agriculture Coalition, "2018 Farm Bill by the Numbers," December 21, 2018, https://sustainableagriculture.net/blog/2018-farm-bill-by-the-numbers/.

6. Karl Evers-Hillstrom, "Farm Bill's Corporate Farm Subsidies Remain Intact after Extensive Lobbying," Opensecrets.org, December 14, 2018, https://www.opensecrets.org/news/2018/12/farm-bill-corporate-farm-subsidies-intact-after-lobbying/.

7. Eric Amel et al., "Independent Restaurants Are a Nexus of Small Businesses in the United States and Drive Billions of Dollars of Economic Activity that Is at Risk of Being Lost Due to the Covid-19 Pandemic," Compass Lexecon-Independent Restaurant Coalition White Paper, June 10, 2020, https://media-cdn.getbento.com/accounts/cf190ba55959ba5052ae23ba6d98e6de/media/R903wxAIR JGukLxai2ZB_Report.pdf.

8. Andy Wang, "Because You've Probably Been a Victim of 'Seafood Fraud'—Here's a High-Tech Solution," *The Observer*, March 16, 2017, https://observer.com/2017/03/los-angeles-michael-cimarusti-dock-to-dish-kickstarter-seafood-fraud/.

9. Amy Scattergood, "How a New Dock to Dish System Hopes to Track Your Seafood in Real Time," *Los Angeles Times*, March 10, 2017, https://www.latimes.com/food/dailydish/la-fo-dock-to-dish-seafood-tracking-system-20170309-story.html.

10. Business Research Division, Leeds School of Business, University of Colorado Boulder, "Good Food 100 Restaurants:

2019 Industry Impact Report," Good Food Media Network, 2019, https://goodfoodmedianetwork.org/wp-content/uploads/2019/10/1015_GF100_AR_12.pdf.

11. The Better Fish, "Sara Brito on Why Good Chefs Care About Good Food" (blog), last accessed December 14, 2022, https://www.thebetterfish.com/impact/sara-brito-on-why-good-chefs-care-about-good-food/.

12. Mattie John Bamman, "Portland Burrito Spot Shutters Amid Claims of Cultural Appropriation," *Portland Eater*, May 22, 2017, https://pdx.eater.com/2017/5/22/15677760/portland-kooks-burrito-cultural-appropriation.

13. J. Weston Phippen, "Kill Every Buffalo You Can! Every Buffalo Dead Is an Indian Gone," *The Atlantic*, May 13, 2016, https://www.theatlantic.com/national/archive/2016/05/the-buffalo-killers/482349/.

14. Sara Usha Maillacheruvu, "The Historical Determinants of Food Insecurity in Native Communities," *Center for Budget and Policy Priorities*, October 4, 2022, https://www.cbpp.org/research/food-assistance/the-historical-determinants-of-food-insecurity-in-native-communities.

15. Allison Herrera, "Indigenous Chefs Are Trying to 'De-Colonize' American Diets," Scripps News, February 2, 2022, https://scrippsnews.com/stories/indigenous-chefs-are-trying-to-de-colonize-american-diets/.

16. Fred de Sam Lazaro, "Traditional Native Foods Are the Key Ingredient in the Sioux Chef's Healthy Cooking," *PBS News Hour*, October 16, 2019, https://www.pbs.org/newshour/show/traditional-native-foods-are-the-key-ingredient-in-the-sioux-chefs-healthy-cooking.

17. Brenna Houck, "Sean Sherman Is Decolonizing American Food," *Eater*, September 1, 2020, https://www.eater.com/21402908/indigenous-food-lab-sean-sherman-sioux-chef-interview.

18. Beth Han, "Suicidal Ideation, Suicide Attempt, and Occupations among Employed Adults Aged 18–64 Years in the United States," *Comprehensive Psychiatry* 66 (April 2016): 176–86, https://doi.org/10.1016/j.comppsych.2016.02.001.

19. Hannah Wallace, "Hard-Knocks Restaurant Workers Are Embracing Mental Wellness," *Reasons to Be Cheerful*, November 13, 2020, https://reasonstobecheerful.world/mental -health-restaurant-workers-covid-sacramento/.

20. Kim Severson et al., "Anthony Bourdain, Renegade Chef Who Reported from the World's Tables, Is Dead at 61," *New York Times*, June 18, 2018, https://www.nytimes.com/ 2018/06/08/business/media/anthony-bourdain-dead .html.

21. Brad Dress, "CDC Says Suicides Peaked in 2018," *The Hill*, March 3, 2022, https://thehill.com/policy/healthcare/596689 -cdc-says-suicides-peaked-in-2018/.

22. J. Ama Mantey, "After Bourdain, Mobilizing to Create a Safety Net for Chefs," *Civil Eats*, March 6, 2019, https:// civileats.com/2019/03/06/after-bourdain-mobilizing-to -create-a-safety-net-for-chefs/.

23. Patrick Mulvaney, as told to author on Zoom interview, March 11, 2022.

24. Mulvaney, interview.

25. Mulvaney, interview.

26. Mulvaney, interview.

27. Jenny Dorsey, as told to author on Zoom interview, November, 19, 2021.

28. Dorsey, interview.

29. Edward Lee and Lindsey Ofcacek, as told to author on Zoom interview, January 18, 2022.

30. National Restaurant Association, "2022 DEI Survey Report," July 11, 2022, https://restaurant.org/research-and-media/ research/research-reports/DEI?utm_source=press&utm

_medium=press&utm_campaign=elevate&utm_content =assoc.

31. Ashlen Wilder, "The State of Women in the Restaurant Industry (2022)," Lunchbox, March 18, 2022, https:// lunchbox.io/learn/restaurant-news/women-in-restaurants -history.

32. Lee and Ofcacek, interview.

33. Lee and Ofcacek, interview.

34. Lee and Ofcacek, interview.

35. Lee and Ofcacek, interview.

36. Michel Nischan, as told to author on Zoom interview, March 2, 2021.

37. National Institute of Food and Agriculture, Gus Schumacher Nutrition Incentive Program, https://www.nifa.usda .gov/grants/programs/hunger-food-security-programs/gus -schumacher-nutrition-incentive-program.

38. Nischan, interview.

39. Francesca Hong, "My Career in Restaurants Taught Me What Local Government Really Needs," *Bon Appétit*, September 14, 2021, https://www.bonappetit.com/story/heads -of-the-table-francesca-hong.

40. Chellie Pingree, "What's for Dinner," American University, Sine Institute for Politics and Policy, January 30, 2020.

41. Bank of America, The 2018 U.S. Trust® Study of High Net Worth Philanthropy, https://www.michiganfoundations .org/system/files/documents/2021-10/high-net-worth2018 .pdf.

42. Charleen Badman, as told to author on Zoom interview, February 6, 2022.

43. US Department of Agriculture, "Food Waste FAQs," accessed May 3, 2023, https://www.usda.gov/foodwaste/faqs.

44. Jean Buzby, "Food Waste and Its Links to Greenhouse Gases and Climate Change," USDA, January 24, 2022, https://

www.usda.gov/media/blog/2022/01/24/food-waste-and-its
-links-greenhouse-gases-and-climate-change.

45. "Restaurant Food Waste Is Killing Your Profit Margin—
Here's How to Fix It" (blog), Notch, October 20, 2018,
https://www.notch.financial/blog/restaurant-food-waste
-profit-margin.

46. Buzby, "Food Waste."

47. Steven Satterfield, as told to author on Zoom interview,
February 11, 2022.

48. Satterfield, interview.

49. KTUV, "San Francisco Michelin Star Chef Fights Food
Waste," KTVU-Fox 2, June 2, 2016, https://www.ktvu.com/
news/san-francisco-michelin-star-chef-fights-food-waste.

50. Tiffany Derry, as told to author, June 2018.

Chapter 3

1. Maria Hines, interview with author on Zoom, July 14, 2021.

2. Anna Kramer, "These Ten Companies Make a Lot of the
Food We Buy," Oxfam, December 14, 2014, https://www
.oxfamamerica.org/explore/stories/these-10-companies
-make-a-lot-of-the-food-we-buy-heres-how-we-made
-them-better/.

3. "True Cost of Food: School Meals Case Study," Center for
Good Food Purchasing and Rockefeller Foundation, November 2021, http://www.rockefellerfoundation.org/report/
true-cost-of-food-school-meals-case-study/.

4. "Critical Concepts," on Dr. Wade W. Nobles's official website, accessed April 10, 2023, https://www.drwadenobles.com/.

5. "Congress and the Public," Congressional Job Approval
chart, Gallup, accessed April 10, 2023, https://news.gallup
.com/poll/1600/congress-public.aspx.

6. "Beyond Distrust: How Americans View Their Government," PEW Research Center, November 23, 2015, https://

www.pewresearch.org/politics/2015/11/23/6-perceptions-of
-elected-officials-and-the-role-of-money-in-politics/.

7. "Food Insecurity among Child (<18 years) Population in the Fredericksburg Regional Foodbank Service
Area," Feeding America, accessed April 10, 2023, https://
map.feedingamerica.org/county/2017/child/virginia/
organization/fredericksburg-regional-foodbank.

8. Joy Crump, interview with author on Zoom, March 19, 2021.

9. "Snap-Eligible Households," Hunger and Health, Feeding
America, accessed May 3, 2023, https://hungerandhealth
.feedingamerica.org/explore-our-work/programs-target
-populations/snap-eligible-households/.

10. The Restaurant Opportunities Center of New York and
the Bay; Food First/Institute for Food and Development
Policy, *Food Insecurity of Restaurant Workers, Food Chain
Workers Alliance,* " July 14, 2014.

11. Crump, interview.

12. Senator Roger Wicker, "Wicker, Sinema, Blumenauer, Fitz-
patrick Introduce the Restaurants Act," press release, June 18,
2020, https://www.wicker.senate.gov/2020/6/wicker-sinema
-blumenauer-fitzpatrick-introduce-the-restaurants-act.

13. "Senate Approves $28.6 Billion Grant for Hospitality,"
Bar and Restaurant, March 8, 2021, https://www.barand
restaurant.com/finances/senate-approves-286-billion-grant
-hospitality.

14. Brett Anderson, "How Small Restaurants Leveraged Their
Pain to Win Stimulus Money," *New York Times*, March 23,
2021.

15. Douglas Hattaway, as told to author, March 2023.

16. Douglas Hattaway, "Achieve Great Things: The Art and
Science of Aspirational Narrative," *Stanford Innovation Review*, April 23, 2014.

17. John Medina, "Brain Rules: Rule 5," https://brainrules.net/short-term-memory/.

18. Medina, "Brain Rules."

19. Allison Davis, "Need to Make Your Message Stick? Do This," Inc.com, accessed April 10, 2023, https://www.inc.com/alison-davis/need-to-make-your-message-stick-science-says-do-this-this-this.html.

20. Independent Restaurant Coalition, talking points and training materials prepared for chefs, June 2020.

21. Cheetie Kumar, Testimony of Cheetie Kumar Chef and Owner of Garland US House of Representatives Committee on Small Business, Subcommittee on Oversight, Investigations, and Regulations, May 27, 2021, https://www.congress.gov/117/meeting/house/112703/witnesses/HHRG-117-SM24-Wstate-KumarC-20210527.pdf.

22. R. E. Petty and P. Briñol, "Persuasion: From Single to Multiple to Metacognitive Processes," *Perspectives on Psychological Science* 3, no. 2 (2008): 137–47, doi:10.1111/j.1745-6916.2008.00071.x.

23. Abraham Maslow, "The Farther Reaches of Human Nature" (New York: Viking, 1971), 269.

24. Earl Blumenauer, "28.6 Billion Restaurant Relief Grant Program Championed by Blumenauer Will Open on May 3," press release, April 27, 2021, https://blumenauer.house.gov/media-center/press-releases/286-billion-restaurant-relief-grant-program-championed-by-blumenauer-will-open-on-may-3.

25. Paul C. Reilly, "Op-Ed: Why Restaurateurs Are Demanding—and Deserve—a Bailout," 5280.com, March 22, 2020, https://www.5280.com/op-ed-why-restaurateurs-are-demanding-and-deserve-a-bailout/.

26. Rachel Nuwer, "Presidential Debates Have Shockingly Little Effect on Election Outcomes," *Scientific American*,

October 20, 2020, https://www.scientificamerican.com/article/presidential-debates-have-shockingly-little-effect-on-election-outcomes/.

27. Michelle Obama, "Remarks by the First Lady at 'Let's Move!' Chefs Event," June 4, 2010, https://obamawhitehouse.archives.gov/the-press-office/remarks-first-lady-lets-move-chefs-event.

28. Barack Obama, "Remarks by the President and First Lady at the Signing of the Healthy, Hunger-Free Kids Act," December 13, 2010. https://obamawhitehouse.archives.gov/the-press-office/2010/12/13/remarks-president-and-first-lady-signing-healthy-hunger-free-kids-act.

Chapter 4

1. Earl Blumenauer, remarks at Chef Action Summit, October 29, 2019, https://www.jamesbeard.org/blog/the-power-of-the-chef-community.

2. Elle Simone Scott, "This Chef's Dream Was Built on SNAP," James Beard Foundation, February 13, 2020, https://www.jamesbeard.org/blog/elle-simone-snap-story.

3. Kwame Onwuachi, interview by author on Zoom, January 18, 2022.

4. Mary Sue Milliken, interview by author on Zoom, January 19, 2022.

5. E. K. Silbergeld, J. Graham, and L. B. Price, "Industrial Food Animal Production, Antimicrobial Resistance, and Human Health," *Annual Review of Public Health* 29 (2008): 151–69, doi:10.1146/annurev.publhealth.29.020907.090904.

6. As cited in Deep Shulka, "Antimicrobial Resistance 'Is Not an Abstract Threat Lurking in the Shadows,'" *Medical News Today*, January 19, 2022, https://www.medicalnewstoday.com/articles/antimicrobial-resistance-is-not-an-abstract-threat-lurking-in-the-shadows.

7. Milliken, interview.

8. Pew Charitable Trusts, "Super Chefs against Superbugs," November 8, 2013, https://www.pewtrusts.org/en/research-and -analysis/articles/2013/11/08/superchefs-against-superbugs.

9. Milliken, interview.

10. The White House, "Executive Order—Combating Antibiotic-Resistant Bacteria," September 18, 2014, https:// obamawhitehouse.archives.gov/the-press-office/2014/09/ 18/executive-order-combating-antibiotic-resistant-bacteria.

11. Milliken, interview.

12. Tom Colicchio, interview by author on Zoom, February 7, 2022.

13. "Undocumented Immigrants' State and Local Tax Contributions," Institute on Taxation and Economic Policy, March 1, 2017, https://itep.org/undocumented-immigrants -state-local-tax-contributions-2017/.

14. Aric Jenkins, "How the Restaurant Industry Is Fighting President Trump on Immigration," *Fortune*, April 10, 2017, https://fortune.com/2017/04/10/restaurant-industry-donald -trump-immigration/.

15. Ashley Hoffman, "'We Cannot Be Taken for Granted.' Chef José Andrés on a Day Without Immigrants," *Time*, February 16, 2017, https://time.com/4672858/day-without -immigrant-strike-jose-andres/.

16. "City Recognizes 'A Day Without Immigrants,'" Office of Immigrant Affairs, Office of the Mayor, City of Philadelphia, May, 17, 2017, https://www.phila.gov/press-releases/ office-of-immigrant-affairs/city-recognizes-a-day-without -immigrants/.

17. Andrea Reusing, interview by author on Zoom, January 31, 2022.

18. US Department of Agriculture, "Food Prices and Spending," Food Expenditure Series, Economic Research Service,

accessed April 10, 2023, https://www.ers.usda.gov/data
-products/ag-and-food-statistics-charting-the-essentials/
food-prices-and-spending/?topicId=2b168260-a717-4708
-a264-cb354e815c67.

19. US Bureau of Labor Statistics, "Occupational Employment
and Wages, May 2021 51-3099 Food Processing Workers, All
Other," accessed April 10, 2023, https://www.bls.gov/oes/
current/oes513099.htm.

20. Judd H. Michael and Serap Gorucu, "Severe Injuries from
Product Movement in the U.S. Food Supply Chain," *Journal
of Safety Research*, 2023, https://doi.org/10.1016/j.jsr.2023.02
.007.

21. Reusing, interview.

22. No Kid Hungry, "AAPI Heritage Month: Interview with
Chef Tim Ma, Cofounder of Chefs Stopping AAPI Hate"
(blog), May 10, 2022, https://www.nokidhungry.org/blog/
aapi-heritage-month-interview-chef-tim-ma-cofounder
-chefs-stopping-aapi-hate.

23. No Kid Hungry, "AAPI Heritage Month."

24. Colicchio, interview.

25. Colicchio, interview.

26. Milliken, interview.

27. Duskie Estes, interview by author on Zoom, October 28,
2021.

28. Estes, interview.

29. Estes, interview.

30. Estes, interview.

Chapter 5

1. Kristopher Moon, interview by author on Zoom, January 24, 2022.

2. Meaghan Yuen, "Social Media Users in the World (2021–
2025)," *Insider Intelligence*, May 11, 2022, https://www.insider

intelligence.com/charts/social-media-users-worldwide-per
-network/.

3. "The Most Surprising Restaurant Social Media Statistics
and Trends in 2023," Qitnux (blog), April 12, 2023, https://
blog.gitnux.com/restaurant-social-media-statistics/.

4. Elise Taylor, "What Makes Food Go Viral," *Vogue*, March 1,
2021, https://www.vogue.com/article/what-makes-a-food-go
-viral-inside-the-explosive-popularity-of-tiktoks-feta-pasta.

5. Julia Moskin, "The Island Is Idyllic. As a Workplace, It's
Toxic." *New York Times*, April 27, 2021, https://www.nytimes
.com/2021/04/27/dining/blaine-wetzel-willows-inn-lummi
-island-abuse.html.

6. Adam Reiner, The Restaurant Manifesto (@restofesto),
Twitter, April 28, 2021, https://twitter.com/restofesto/status/
1387268359666999296?s=20.

7. Jackie Varrriano, "The Willows Inn on Lummi Island Set-
tles $1.37 Million Class-Action Wage Theft Lawsuit," *Seat-
tle Times*, October 15, 2022 (last updated October 16, 2022),
https://www.seattletimes.com/life/food-drink/the-willows
-inn-on-lummi-island-settles-1-37-million-class-action
-wage-theft-lawsuit/.

8. PEW Research Center, "Americans Spending More Time
Following the News," September 12, 2010, https://www
.pewresearch.org/politics/2010/09/12/americans-spending
-more-time-following-the-news/.

9. Sprout Social, "50+ of the Most Important Social Media
Marketing Statistics for 2023," March 23, 2023, https://
sproutsocial.com/insights/social-media-statistics/.

10. Adele Peters, "Most Millennials Would Take a Pay Cut to
Work at an Environmentally Responsible Company," *Fast
Company*, February 14, 2019, https://www.fastcompany.com/
90306556/most-millennials-would-take-a-pay-cut-to-work
-at-a-sustainable-company.

11. TextSanity, "SMS Open Rates: How Often Do People Open Marketing Texts?," July 14, 2022, https://textsanity.com/text-message-marketing/sms-open-rates/.

12. Moon, interview.

13. Jenny Dorsey, interview by author on Zoom, November 19, 2021.

14. Linda Chestney, "A Medium for Social Change," *Artscope*, January/February 2016, https://artscopemagazine.com/2016/01/a-medium-for-social-change/.

15. Haley Britzky, "#MeToo Hashtag Used over 19 Million Times on Twitter," *Axios*, October 13, 2018, https://www.axios.com/2018/10/13/metoo-hashtag-used-over-19-million-times-on-twitter.

16. Wynne Davis, "Bakers Against Racism Aims to Fight Injustice with the Power of Food," NPR, June 20, 2020, https://www.npr.org/2020/06/20/881075595/bakers-against-racism-aims-to-fight-injustice-with-the-power-of-food.

17. Bakers Against Racism, "Our History," accessed April 14, 2023, https://www.bakersagainstracism.com.

18. Paola Velez, interview by author on Zoom, January 28, 2022.

19. Velez, interview.

20. Velez, interview.

21. Velez, interview.

22. Meghan McCarron, "Bakers Against Racism Is Just the Beginning," *Eater*, June 18, 2020, https://www.eater.com/2020/6/18/21295842/bakers-against-racism-bake-sale-instagram-movement-black-lives-matter.

23. Klancy Miller, "Overlooked No More: Georgia Gilmore, Who Fed and Funded the Montgomery Bus Boycott," *New York Times*, July 31, 2019, https://www.nytimes.com/2019/07/31/obituaries/georgia-gilmore-overlooked.html.

24. Daniella Byck, "DC Pastry Chefs Launch a National Bake Sale to Support Black Lives Matter," *Washingtonian*,

June 5, 2020, https://www.washingtonian.com/2020/06/05/
dc-pastry-chefs-launch-a-national-bake-sale-to-support
-black-lives-matter/.

25. Rick Reilly, "Nothing But Nets," *Sports Illustrated*, May 1,
2006, https://vault.si.com/vault/2006/05/01/nothing-but
-nets.

26. Margaret McDonnell, "A New Era of Nothing But Nets:
United to Beat Malaria," *UN Foundation*, March 14, 2022,
https://unfoundation.org/blog/post/a-new-era-of-nothing
-but-nets-united-to-beat-malaria/.

27. Annenberg Public Policy Center, "Americans Support
GMO Food Labels but Don't Know Much about Safety of GM Foods," July 18, 2016, https://www.annenberg
publicpolicycenter.org/americans-support-gmo-food
-labels-but-dont-know-much-about-safety-of-genetically
-modified-foods/.

28. Samantha Falewée, "Protecting Health or Spreading Fear?
The Battle over GMO Labeling Goes National," *Wine
Spectator*, March 30, 2016, https://www.winespectator.com/
articles/protecting-health-or-spreading-fear-the-battle
-over-gmo-labeling-goes-national-52942.

29. Scott Wise, "Why These Richmond Chefs Are Pushing for
GMO Labels on Food," *CBS-6 News Richmond*, October 22,
2015, https://www.wtvr.com/2015/10/22/richmond-chefs
-gmo-labeling.

30. Jenny Splitter, "How a Decade of GMO Controversy
Changed the Dialogue about Food," *Forbes*, December 20,
2019, https://www.forbes.com/sites/jennysplitter/2019/12/
20/how-a-decade-of-gmo-controversy-changed-the
-dialogue-about-food/?sh=1e7b9bba6434.

31. Preeti Mistry, "I'm a Queer Brown Immigrant Chef. I Don't
Have the Luxury of Staying Silent," *Time*, February 7, 2019,
https://time.com/5520560/chef-preeti-mistry-activism/.

32. Velez, interview.
33. Clint Rainey, "This Restaurant Duo Want a Zero-Carbon Food System. Can It Happen?," *MIT Technology Review*, September 24, 2020, https://www.technologyreview.com/2020/09/24/1008724/carbon-farming-myint-leibowitz-mission-chinese-zero-foodprint-climate-change/.
34. Ray Levy Uyeda, "Zero Foodprint Founder Anthony Myint Talks to Chef Daniel Asher About Regenerative Agriculture and More," *Plate*, July 17, 2022, https://plateonline.com/chefs-and-restaurants/zero-foodprint-founder-anthony-myint-talks-chef-daniel-asher-about.
35. Green America, "Restaurants Are Helping to Drive Carbon Farming Practices," https://www.greenamerica.org/story/zero-foodprint.
36. Moon, interview.

Chapter 6

1. Preeti Mistry, interview by author on Zoom, January 21, 2022.
2. Yea-Hung Chen et al., "Excess Mortality Associated with the COVID-19 Pandemic among Californians 18–65 Years of Age, by Occupational Sector and Occupation: March through October 2020," doi:https://doi.org/10.1101/2021.01.21.21250266.
3. Feeding America, "The Impact of Coronavirus on Food Insecurity," accessed April 28, 2023, https://www.feedingamerica.org/research/coronavirus-hunger-research.
4. Economic Policy Institute Minimum Wage Tracker, last accessed February 19, 2023, https://go.epi.org/gxpJ.
5. Holl Petre, "What Does $15 per Hour Minimum Wage in Florida Mean for Restaurants?," *National Restaurant News*, November 9, 2020, https://www.nrn.com/fast-casual/what-does-15-hour-minimum-wage-florida-mean-restaurants.

6. Restaurant Opportunities Center United, "2020 State of Restaurant Workers," accessed April 28, 2023, https://stateof restaurantworkers.com/.

7. Mary Yagoda, "Restaurant Workers Call for End to Tipped Minimum Wage," *Yahoo! News*, June 26, 2018, https://sports .yahoo.com/restaurant-workers-call-end-tipped-190633361 .html.

8. Amanda Cohen, "Restaurant Owners Should Embrace—and Pay Above—the $15 Minimum Wage," *Eater*, September 6, 2019, https://www.eater.com/2019/9/6/20849277/higher -minimum-wage-15-good-for-restaurant-owners-employees.

9. Ryan Knutson and Kate Linebaugh, "One Restaurant Owner's Answer to the Labor Shortage," *The Journal*, September 30, 2021, https://www.wsj.com/podcasts/the-journal/ one-restaurant-owner-answer-to-the-labor-shortage/ 7477ff7e-f766-4e7f-b02f-36efbf122731.

10. Renee Erickson, interview by author on Zoom, February 7, 2022.

11. Open Secrets, "National Restaurant Association, Summary (multiple years)," accessed April 28, 2023, https://www .opensecrets.org/orgs/national-restaurant-assn/summary ?id=D000000150.

12. Office of Senator Elizabeth Warren, "Senators Warren, Sanders, Murray Push National Restaurant Association for Answers Following Bombshell Report of Misuse of Food Safety Training Funds," press release, February 6, 2023, https://www.warren.senate.gov/newsroom/press-releases/ senators-warren-sanders-murray-push-national-restaurant -association-for-answers-following-bombshell-report-of -misuse-of-food-safety-training-funds.

13. B Corp, "The Legal Requirement for Certified B Corporations," accessed April 28, 2023, https://www.bcorporation .net/en-us/about-b-corps/legal-requirements.

14. Tess Hart, interview by author on Zoom, April 9, 2022.
15. Dustin Walsh, "No Secrets: Businesses Find It Pays to Open Books to Employees," *Crain's Detroit Business*, January 17, 2010, https://www.zingermanscommunity.com/2010/01/the-secrets-of-open-book-finanace/.
16. Maddie Oatman, "Can Co-ops Save Restaurants?," *Mother Jones*, May–June 2021, https://www.motherjones.com/food/2021/04/can-co-ops-save-restaurants/.
17. Oscar Perry Abello, "Now Is the Time to Re-Think Everything about How Food Businesses Work," Shareable.com, September 10, 2020, https://www.shareable.net/re-thinking-how-food-businesses-work/.
18. Brenna Houck, "Food Is Political. It's a Part of Our DNA," *Eater*, September 21, 2020, https://www.eater.com/21432753/devita-davison-interview-foodlab-detroit-future-of-food-world-restaurants.
19. Houck, "Food Is Political."
20. Elena Kadvanvy, "Worker-Owned Bay Area Businesses Are on the Rise," *San Francisco Chronicle*, February 21, 2022, https://www.sfchronicle.com/food/article/Worker-owned-Bay-Area-food-businesses-are-on-the-16930344.php.
21. Rep. Jim McGovern, "McGovern, Newhouse, Pingree, Walorski Introduce New Bipartisan Bill to Increase Food Donations and Prevent Hunger," press release, December 13, 2021, https://mcgovern.house.gov/news/documentsingle.aspx?DocumentID=398774.
22. We Don't Waste, "Why Congress Should Pass the Food Donation Improvement Act," WeDon'tWaste.com, July 22, 2022, https://www.wedontwaste.org/why-congress-should-pass-the-food-donation-improvement-act/#:~:text=Chef%20and%20advocate%20Tom%20Colicchio,are%20responsible%20for%20feeding%20us.%E2%80%9D.

23. The White House, "Bills Signed," press release, January 5, 2023. https://www.whitehouse.gov/briefing-room/legislation/2023/01/05/press-release-bills-signed-h-r-680-h-r-897-h-r-1082-h-r-1154-h-r-1917-h-r-7939-s-450-s-989-s-1294-s-1402-s-1541-s-1942-s-2333-s-2834-s-3168-s-3308-s-3405-s-35/.

24. Mary Sue Milliken, interview by author on Zoom, January 19, 2022.

25. United Nations, "Our Growing Population," accessed May 4, 2023, https://www.un.org/en/global-issues/population.

26. Food Is Life: The Chefs' Manifesto, accessed April 28, 2023, https://sdg2advocacyhub.org/chefs-manifesto.

27. William Dissen, as told to author, January 20, 2021.

28. World Food Programme, "U.N. World Food Programme Announces Andrew Zimmern as Goodwill Ambassador," press release, December 6, 2021. https://www.wfp.org/news/un-world-food-programme-announces-andrew-zimmern-goodwill-ambassador.

29. Rick LeBlanc, "Why the U.S. Wastes More Food than Almost Any Other Country," Liveabout.com, June 25, 2019, https://www.liveabout.com/food-waste-greater-in-us-than-almost-all-countries-4164313#:~:text=The%20U.S.%20was%20recently%20ranked,at%20361%20kg%20per%20capita.

30. Kylie Kwong, "Kylie Kwong on Food Waste and How We Can Curb It," *Foodwise*, accessed April 10, 2023, https://www.foodwise.com.au/food-waste-we-can-curb-it/.

31. Everytown for Gun Safety, "Mass Shootings," accessed April 28, 2023, https://www.everytown.org/issues/mass-shootings/.

32. Peter Romero, "FBI Ranks Restaurants as 8th Most Common Setting for Violent Crime," *Restaurant Business*, September 27, 2021, https://www.restaurantbusinessonline.com/operations/fbi-ranks-restaurants-8th-most-common-setting-violent-crime#:~:text=FBI%20ranks%20restaurants

%20as%208th%20most%20common%20setting%20for%20
violent%20crime,-Eating%20and%20drinking&text=At
%20least%2010%2C490%20violent%20crimes,released%20
Monday%20by%20the%20FBI.

33. Anonymous, as told to author, February 14, 2023.

34. Jeanne O'Brien Coffey, "Boston Chefs Cook Up a Dinner to Support Gun Safety," *Forbes*, September, 30, 2019, https://www.forbes.com/sites/jeanneobriencoffey/2019/09/30/boston-chefs-cook-up-a-dinner-to-support-gun-safety/?sh=1b991ef51143.

35. Dominique Crenn, acceptance speech at James Beard Foundation Awards, May 7, 2018.

36. José Andrés, acceptance speech at James Beard Foundation Awards, May 7, 2018.

37. Andrés, acceptance speech.

Index

Entries for tables and textboxes are noted in italics.

215

About the Author

Called one of the most innovative women in food and beverage by *Fortune* and *Food & Wine* magazines, Katherine Miller is a past vice president of impact at the James Beard Foundation and the founding executive director of the Chef Action Network. She was the first-ever

Photo by Brooks Craft

food policy fellow at American University's Sine Institute for Policy and Politics and served as a Distinguished Terker Fellow at George Washington University. She founded Table 81 and works directly with chefs, philanthropists, foundations, and socially responsible businesses to create policy advocacy and social change campaigns. She is also an adjunct professor at the Culinary Institute of America. She is a past board member of RAINN, the national sexual assault hotline, and NARAL ProChoice America. She is a member of Les Dames d'Escoffier and on the board of directors of the New Venture Fund. Miller lives on the ancestral lands of the Anocostans in Northeast Washington, DC, with her husband, Lou, and their kitty, Lily.